PRINT CASEBOOKS 7/1987-88 EDITION
THE BEST IN ADVERTISING

Print
Casebooks 7
1987/1988

The Best in
Advertising

Written by
Tom Goss

Published by
**RC Publications, Inc.
Bethesda, MD**

AAV 8938

Introduction

Published by RC Publications, Inc.
6400 Goldsboro Road
Bethesda, MD 20817

Manufactured in U.S.A.
First Printing 1986

PRINT CASEBOOKS 7/1987-88 EDITION/THE BEST IN ADVERTISING
Library of Congress Catalog Card Number 75-649579
ISBN 0-915734-48-6

PRINT CASEBOOKS 7/1987-88 EDITION
Complete 6-Volume Set
ISBN 0-915734-47-8
3-Volume Set
ISBN 0-915734-54-0

RC PUBLICATIONS
President and Publisher: Howard Cadel
Vice President and Editor: Martin Fox
Creative Director: Andrew P. Kner
Managing Editor: Teresa Reese
Art Director: Scott Menchin
Associate Editor: Tom Goss
Graphic Production: Jung Hyang Kim
Video Consultant: Loretta Tassotti

One evening in the autumn of 1985, five advertising professionals representing the industry's different creative roles of art director, copywriter and producer gathered at the editorial offices of PRINT magazine in New York City to examine the field of over 1800 entries to the seventh edition of *Print Casebooks: The Best in Advertising* competition. By the end of the evening, the five professionals had chosen 50 winners—a mix of individual print ads, print campaigns, individual TV spots, TV campaigns, plus a print/TV combination and several outdoor campaigns.

During the dinner break that followed part of the television judging and all of the print, the jurors were asked for their observations on what they had seen so far. They all agreed that though, as one juror put it, "there's a lot of competent work out there," the field of entries offered little "to get excited about." "There are no new ideas," that same juror commented, "nothing in the way of innovation. It's as if everyone just said, 'Let's go for the clever line.'"

Indeed, another juror remarked that, in print at least, the vehicle of humor to convey the client's message was apparently being over-used. "There seemed to be a lot of headlines with jokes in them that were simply in poor taste," he observed. "They were otherwise well-constructed, but the humor was inappropriate to the subject matter."

"I noticed a lot of that in ads for hospitals and medical services," a third juror agreed. "They would try to make a pun on some awful disease."

The obsessive reliance on humor, or attempts at humor, the jurors concurred, could be traced to the continued success of the Minneapolis agency, Fallon McElligott Rice. "I saw *a lot* of ads that looked like Fallon McElligott knock-offs," a juror observed. "They had the same tightly stacked caps and the large visual. They were very clean looking, but the copy just wasn't as sharp."

"It's as if the whole creative part of the industry was solving all their clients' problems in the same way instead of different ways," added another juror.

Though, indeed, Fallon McElligott Rice is the closest thing there is to a big winner in the print category, having earned the inclusion of four campaigns, the remaining print ads selected for this *Casebook* represent a wide cross section of original and creative advertising from around the country. Included here as well are Ally and Gargano's striking and surreal campaign for Karastan Carpets, Chiat/Day's vividly graphic campaign for IBM typewriters, Lawler Ballard's appropriately serious ad for Norfolk General Hospital, Martin/William's clever trade ad for 3M Office Supplies Division, and Salisbury Communications' freewheeling and playful campaign for Gotcha Sportswear. Outdoor advertising is also well-represented by the jury's selections: Holland and Calloway's poster campaign for New York radio station WNEW-AM, Levine Huntley Schmidt and Beaver's combination print and outdoor campaign for McCall's magazine, and James

A. Jacobs, Inc.'s fire-ravaged billboard for Frederick Rauh and Co. insurance, which once again proves that the medium is the message.

One group of ads selected by the *Casebook* jury stands out for its unique and beautiful visual vocabulary. Though executed for the most part by different agencies for different clients, the common thread tying these ads together is their audience of affluent, health- and fitness-conscious consumers. Most of these ads are for exercise equipment—Wieden and Kennedy's for Nike and Soloflex and Fallon McElligott's for AMF Heavy Hands—and use the talents of photographer Dennis Manarchy to give their potentially gritty subjects a classical grace and elegance. Though not an exercise product, Pabst Light beer was meant to appeal to the same audience, and Young and Rubicam/Chicago's campaign, therefore, cleverly used the same visual approach, though not the same photographer.

It was quite clear from the jurors' comments over dinner and during the subsequent screening of the remaining television entries that they unanimously felt the television to be superior overall to the print. "I think this is simply because the talented people who have been working for a while are put into TV, which represents more money," one juror explained. "There doesn't seem as much effort put into print work as there is into TV."

"You can't put an ad on your reel," another wryly agreed.

Also apparent from the judging is the fact that director Joe Sedelmaier remains a strong

influence on the character of television advertising, as he continues to leave his indelible stamp on commercials for a wide variety of agencies and clients. "The amazing thing about Sedelmaier," a juror observed, "is that he does a lot of work and so much of it is good. He's practically created his own genre."

"But do people remember who those jokes are for?" another juror wondered aloud. "He seems more interested in his own style than in creating a memorable style for the clients."

"I imagine that his commercials do well in spite of that because of what's out there on the air," still another juror opined. "His humor is so outrageous that it can't help but be noticed."

Whatever the reservations expressed by some of the jurors, four campaigns directed by the funny man from Chicago are included in this *Casebook*: Livingston and Company's campaign for Alaska Airlines (marking its second *Casebook* appearance), Campbell-Ewald Canada's campaign for Owens Corning Fiberglas Pink, Della Femina Travisano's campaign for Kaypro Computers, and Dancer Fitzgerald Sample's now-legendary campaign for Wendy's Restaurants.

Completely unreserved were the jurors' endorsements of BBDO's campaigns for Pepsi and Diet Pepsi, the latter being the only campaign in either print or television to be singled out by the jury as breaking new ground. One juror remarked that Adrian Lyne, the director who set the style and tone of the Pepsi campaign, though he

didn't direct all the individual spots, "did for TV advertising what Tony Scott did when he introduced the 'new wave' several years ago for the same client." "Now, everyone's shooting commercials with tight close-ups and intimate settings," she observed.

The current trend in the advertising industry to follow the few innovators, rather than innovate, was lamented more than once during the evening, leading one juror to conclude that "it's not a terrifically creative time in advertising." He expressed some hope for better times, however, by citing a talk given by writer and cultural pundit Tom Wolfe at the 1985 American Institute of Graphic Arts conference in Boston. "Wolfe said that the only two original and innovative art forms of the 20th century are art-direction and the movies—nothing else is breaking new ground," the juror recalled. "If that's true, then the fact that TV commercials represent a combination of those two forms means that there is potential for some very exciting work."—*Tom Goss*

Casebook Writer

Tom Goss

Associate editor of PRINT since 1985, Tom Goss received his B.A. in American Literature from Ramapo State College of New Jersey in 1979. He joined PRINT in 1982 as an editorial assistant and was promoted to assistant editor shortly thereafter. In addition to his work for PRINT, Goss is contributing editor to PRINT's sister publication, HOW, and the writer of *Casebooks 6: The Best in Advertising.*

Casebook Jurors

Mark Hughes

A graduate of the Art Center College of Design in Pasadena, California, Mark Hughes joined Doyle Dane Bernbach, New York, as an assistant art director in 1980. Two years later, he became an art director, and shortly thereafter, an art supervisor. He became an agency vice-president in 1984, and in 1985 was promoted to his current position of vice-president and associate creative director. Throughout his tenure at DDB, Hughes has worked for such clients as Volkswagen, Clairol, Colombian Coffee, Chivas Regal, Paine Webber and Weight Watchers. In addition to winning many awards, Hughes was named one of the "100 best and brightest young people in advertising" by Advertising Age in 1985.

Lynne Kluger

Lynne Kluger is senior vice-president and director of the Broadcast Department of Avrett, Free and Ginsberg, Inc. Before joining this New York agency, she spent five years as head of TV production at Della Femina Travisano and Partners in Los Angeles. She has produced many award-winning commercials for such clients as Ralston Purina Co., Carter Wallace, Inc., and PSA Airlines of Los Angeles.

Andrew Kner

Born in Hungary, where his family had been involved in design since the 18th century, Andrew Kner came to the U.S. in 1940 at the age of five. He received his B.A. from Yale in 1957 and his M.F.A. in 1959. He worked in promotion design for Esquire and Look magazines, then joined the New York Times where he served for a year as art director of the Sunday Book Review. In 1970, he became art director of the Times's promotion department, a position he held till 1984, when he moved to Backer and Spielvogel as creative director of the agency's Promotion Group. He has also been art director of PRINT since 1962. Kner teaches at Parsons and at the Rhode Island School of Design. He was president of the New York Art Directors Club from 1983 to 1985.

Steven Landsberg

Currently a senior copywriter at McCann-Erickson, New York, Steven Landsberg attended the School of Visual Arts where he studied art direction and copywriting. After graduating from SVA with honors in 1980, he spent four and a half years with Doyle Dane Bernbach working on accounts for Volkswagen, IBM, Chivas Regal, and Atari, among others. After leaving DDB, Landsberg joined, first, Calet, Hirsch and Spector, then Chiat/Day New York, where his accounts included Glenfiddich Scotch, Christian Dior and NYNEX. His work has earned him awards from the New York Art Directors Show and the One Show, as well as Andies, Clios and Athenas. His work has also been published in Graphis, PRINT, the *Print Casebooks* and CA.

Jack Tauss

Currently senior vice-president of Jerry Fields-Group 2, the art and graphic design search affiliate of Jerry Fields Associates, Inc., the communications personnel recruitment firm, Jack Tauss has had wide experience as an art director with several advertising agencies and with his own design firm, Concorde Associates. In addition to his work in advertising, he has done stints as creative director of Macmillan Publishing and creative director of The Franklin Mint/Franklin Library Division, which he left to join Jerry Fields Associates. Active in professional organizations, Tauss served as president of the Type Directors Club and secretary of the New York Art Directors Club. He has won over 50 awards from these and other art and graphic design groups.

Clients/Products

Agencies

Dayton's/Kenzo
For Spring

Dayton's is a midwestern chain of department stores, similar to Macy's of New York and San Francisco. Like many such stores located in large cities, the Minneapolis branch has a boutique within the store itself which caters to those fashion-conscious customers with the means to pay for original designs. Called the Oval Room, the boutique in the Minneapolis store became the showcase for a line of spring clothing designed by the Japanese coutourier Kenzo in late January of 1985. To publicize that event, Dayton's in-house art director, Robert Valentine, was instructed to "design an image piece to make the Oval Room customer aware that we were carrying Kenzo as part of our Oval Room spring inventory. "Since the merchandise was new for the Oval Room," Valentine says, "I wanted the ad to look current and fresh in terms of the treatment of color and type styles."

Originally, Valentine wanted the ad, which was to run in local magazines, to consist of two pages: one on which a color photograph of the merchandise was to appear alone, and a vellum overlay which was to carry the type. "I had seen a paper sample book done by Alan Cober," Valentine recalls. "He had printed on vellum with rubber stamps and had sketched over the letters. Unfortunately, doing the same with our ad would have meant pre-printing the vellum and inserting it over the regular ad, which wasn't possible because of magazine specifications and publication deadlines."

Many of Valentine's ideas

made it into the ad, nonetheless. The ad, with its hand-drawn rules, hand-stamped type, bright rules and informal layout, is the very essence of spring. "Another factor in the design was the store's theme of 'prints,'" Valentine says of the hand-stamped type. "I wanted to

carry that through by giving the impression of something stamped right on the page."

Valentine says he is unaware of any research conducted to determine the ad's effect on the Oval Room's sales. He adds, however, that the single-page ad "has been a consistent winner for us in design shows."

Client: Dayton Hudson Department Store, Minneapolis
Agency: In-house
Art director: Robert Valentine
Copywriter: Vicky Rossi
Photographer: Charles Tracy

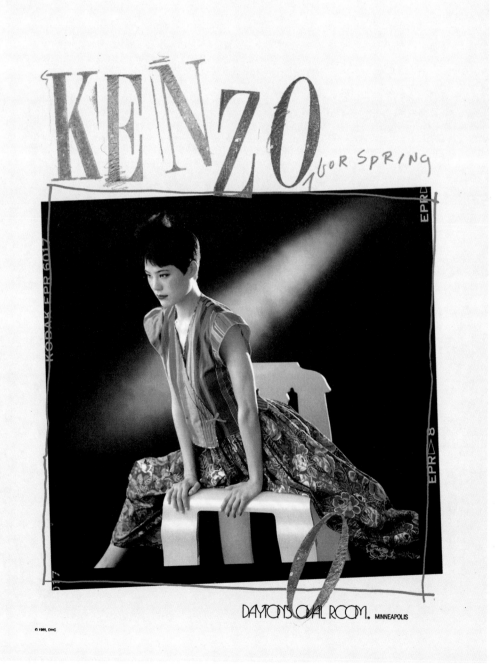

American Honda Scooters

Already a market leader in the sale of motorcycles and cars, Honda wanted to tap a younger market with the introduction of lower-cost motor scooters. "What we had to do," says Wieden and Kennedy account executive Steve Keenan, "was present scooters as a contemporary form of transportation for people who aren't afraid to be different." The challenge of that approach, Keenan notes, "was that we were talking to people who categorically marched to their own drummer." "Jim Riswold,

the copywriter," he continues, "is a big Lou Reed fan, and he thought Reed would make a good spokesman. Fortunately for us, Reed wanted to do the spot from the outset."

The resulting 60-second spot is something of a Lou Reed rock video. Using his popular song "Walk on the Wild Side" as the soundtrack, the commercial depicts a series of New York street scenes in which a sharp-eyed observer would pick out several Honda scooters. It ends as the camera finds Reed sitting on a scooter in front of New

York's famous nightclub, the Bottom Line. "Hey," Reed says as a traffic signal above his head flashes DON'T WALK, "don't settle for walking."

The commercial began running in 1985 on a national basis, and continued to run on into 1986. Keenan describes response to the spot as very positive. "Consumer awareness of Honda scooters has jumped considerably," he says. "And the press has reported sales increases as high as 85 per cent."

Client: American Honda Motor Co., Inc.
Agency: Wieden & Kennedy, Portland, OR
Art director: Rick McQuiston
Copywriter: Jim Riswold
Production company: Steve Horn Productions, New York City
Director: Steve Horn

HONDA
SCOOTERS

Lou Reed
60 Seconds
(Music: "Walk on the Wild Side")
Lou Reed: Hey, don't settle
for walking.

Villa Linda Mall

"You can't visit Santa Fe without being influenced by its beautiful setting and by its dedication to the arts," observes Don Sibley, principal of Dallas's Sibley/Peteet, by way of explaining his campaign for the Villa Linda Mall. "After we saw how arts-oriented the community was," he recalls, "we knew a sophisticated graphics approach would be appropriate."

The Villa Linda Mall, a development by the Dallas-based real estate developer the Herring Group, opened in Santa Fe's business district in 1985. Sibley's effort was to create a campaign that would "fit the cultural climate of the community" and present the mall as a desirable addition to the city's distinctive ambiance. "The last thing we wanted to do," Sibley says, "was to come off as some big-city developer trying to change a small-town attitude."

Sibley's original plan was to evoke the rich Spanish-American heritage and tradition of Santa Fe, but he abandoned that approach as "lacking emphasis on merchandise." "We wanted to be merchandise-oriented," he explains, "although not too hard-sell."

Indeed, the month-long campaign as it ran in local newspapers looks more like a series of eye-catching posters than it does a series of ads. Filled with bright, saturated colors and unobtrusive copy, the ads depict retail products set against the backdrop of Santa Fe's mountains and desert horizon. "We adopted an art style that, like the community, was sophisticated but casual," Sibley says. "For the emphasis on merchandise, we chose images that were simple, generic symbols of retail categories—fashion, food, gifts and entertainment." The fashion category, he explains, is represented by the shoe, food by the ubiquitous southwestern chili pepper, gifts by the ring, and entertainment by the gaily painted toy.

Sibley says the campaign has been credited with the mall's successful opening. "Initial response and sales figures for the mall," he notes, "are much higher than projected."

Client: The Herring Group
Agency: Sibley/Peteet Design, Inc., Dallas
Art director/copywriter/illustrator: Don Sibley

VILLA LINDA MALL

Top: Comps for early proposal rejected as not putting enough emphasis on merchandise. Right: Comp for "Shoe" ad. Following pages: Finished ads.

Something eventful is on the Santa Fe horizon.

Away we go. This week Villa Linda Mall gets off to a flying start. With lots of color. Lots of razzle-dazzle. And lots of fun for you. It all begins Tuesday afternoon with a "Hare and Hound" hot air balloon race. Don't miss the launch of 20 balloons at 5:30 pm. Then join us for the grand opening celebration Wednesday at 9 am with a ribbon cutting ceremony, climaxed by 6,000 balloons released skyward. Enjoy the day – or the entire week – of exciting events. From marching bands to strolling minstrels. Fashion shows to magic shows. And best of all, enjoy a whole new shopping experience that's more fashionable, more delicious, and more fun than you've ever imagined. So come. See for yourself. The horizon has never looked better.

 VILLA LINDA MALL

Cerrillos at Rodeo Road. Opening July 31, with Dillard's, Mervyn's, and 100 other stores. JCPenney opening summer of 1986.

Something fun is on the Santa Fe horizon.

It's getting close. Villa Linda Mall. Opening

Wednesday, July 31. Discover a whole new shopping

experience that's more fun than you've ever

imagined. Things to do. Things to hear. Things you've

never seen before. From kids' games to grown-ups'

toys. Movies and munchies and many hours of

enjoyable shopping. Everything you've always

wanted. All right here at home in one beautiful mall

reflecting the finest Santa Fe traditions. Over 100

stores and restaurants in all, including Dillard's and

Mervyn's. So come see for yourself. The horizon

has never looked better.

VILLA LINDA MALL

Cerrillos at Rodeo Road. Opening July 31, with Dillard's, Mervyn's, and 100 other stores. JCPenney opening summer of 1986.

Something delicious is on the Santa Fe horizon.

So good, you can almost taste it. El Mercado at

Villa Linda Mall. Opening today at 10am. Treat yourself

to a food fantasyland filled with all your favorite

things to eat. From the hot and spicy to the cool and

creamy. Pizza, pastries, popcorn. Everything

you've ever been hungry for served in a colorful and

festive atmosphere reflecting the finest Santa Fe

traditions. And best of all, it's right in the middle of

the hottest shopping sensation ever. Over 100

stores and restaurants in all, including Dillard's

and Mervyn's. So come see for yourself. The horizon

has never looked better.

VILLA LINDA MALL

Cerrillos at Rodeo Road. Opening July 31, with Dillard's, Mervyn's, and 100 other stores. JCPenney opening summer of 1986.

Today the Santa Fe horizon looks better than ever.

Today at 10 am, discover something different on

the horizon. Villa Linda Mall. A whole new shopping

experience more fashionable, more fun, and

more delicious than you've ever imagined. Over 100

special shops, stores and restaurants, including

Dillard's and Mervyn's. Filled with everything you've

always wanted. From the latest fashions to fine

antiques. Gifts and gadgets galore. The scrumptious,

the luscious, and the humorous. All right here at

home in one beautiful mall reflecting the finest Santa

Fe traditions. So come see for yourself. The horizon

has never looked better.

VILLA LINDA MALL

Cerrillos at Rodeo Road. Dillard's, Mervyn's, and 100 other stores. JCPenney opening summer of 1986.

Something fashionable is on the Santa Fe horizon.

Watch for it. Villa Linda Mall. Opening Wednesday,

July 31. You'll discover a whole new shopping

experience more fashionable than you've ever

imagined. Lots and lots of special shops and stores

filled with all the hottest colors and the latest

styles. From casual to chic. From simple to sensational.

Everything you've always wanted. And all right

here at home in one beautiful mall reflecting the finest

Santa Fe traditions. Over 100 stores and restaurants

in all, including Dillard's and Mervyn's. So come

see for yourself. The horizon has never looked better.

VILLA LINDA MALL

Cerrillos at Rodeo Road. Opening July 31, with Dillard's, Mervyn's, and 100 other stores. JCPenney opening summer of 1986.

Pepsi-Cola

Although the apparent marketing blunder by which Coca-Cola ended up being forced to market two versions of its flagship product would seem ripe material for the advertising of its major competitor, BBDO creative director Harvey Hoffenberg says that the thrust of his ongoing campaign for Pepsi has been to "carve out a niche for Pepsi that is Pepsi's, not Coke's." "The soft-drink market is getting younger," he says, "and the struggle now is to find out who owns this younger generation."

Hoffenberg, while admitting that being a part of this "younger generation" is primarily a "state of mind," defines his campaign's audience as "younger types," aged 12 to 34. "What we try to do," he says, "is to project an image of the product that the kids want to be seen with. We do that by making Pepsi's kids 'hipper' than Coke's kids, and the fact that Coca-Cola came out with 'New Coke' attests to the success of our approach."

One of the ways Hoffenberg seems to have made Pepsi's kids "hipper" is by depicting them as smart and savvy players in the business world. In one 60-second spot ("Soundtruck"), a young entrepreneur uses state-of-the-art technology to lure and hook customers for his soft-drink concession. Pulling his truckload of Pepsi up to a crowded beach full of sweltering sunbathers, the spot's young hero tantalizes his customers with the sounds of an ice-cold Pepsi being poured into a glass, amplifying the sounds with a sophisticated sound system.

Soundtruck
60 Seconds
(**SFX: Beach sounds, i.e., wind and water. Radio D.J. in background. Sounds of speakers being raised atop truck.**
Sounds of ice cubes being dropped into glass. Sound is heard across beach.
Sound of popping top. Sound of **popping top echoes over beach. Sound of popping continues.**
Sound of fizzing soda. Sounds of fizzing soda are heard across beach. Sounds of fizzing continue.
Boy: . . . Aah . . . Okay, who's first?
(**SFX: Crowd noises**)
Anncr: VO: Pepsi. The choice of a new generation.

Once he has his audience's attention, he opens his truck to reveal cases of frosty Pepsi, which he then sells to a crowd of eager, thirsty buyers. Hoffenberg observes that though the campaign's theme is "Pepsi, the choice of a new generation," the choices aspect is more implicit in this spot than in others of the campaign. "The competitive aspect of the choice theme takes place off-camera in this case," he says. "It presents Pepsi as the choice of the spot's clever and aggressive entrepreneur."

In one commercial ("Spaceship"), this competitive aspect of the choice theme becomes quite overt, although in a tongue-in-cheek way. Set at night in a small town, the spot depicts a taste test performed by extraterrestrial visitors who sample a can each of Coke and Pepsi from a pair of roadside vending machines. Though neither the TV viewer nor the boy witnessing the event ever sees the aliens inside the spacecraft, their choice is made clear by the fact that the creatures take the entire Pepsi vending machine with them as they disappear into the night.

Another spot with an equally mischievous sense of humor ("Archeology") is set "sometime in the future." It depicts a college professor taking his class to "the greatest archeological discovery of our time: a dwelling called the split-level ranch." As the class proceeds through the ruin, the students—who are seen sipping from cans of Pepsi—bring various artifacts to the professor for identification—which he provides, though with some humorous distortions.

(SFX: Ominous music. Sounds of boy and dog playing.)
Boy: Fetch, boy.
(SFX: Ominous music. Dog barks. Music gets increasingly louder. Wind, light computer-like sounds. Soothing music.)
Anncr: VO: Pepsi. The choice of a new generation.

When one student finds an object too crusted with dirt to identify, the professor places it in a machine for cleaning. The object is revealed to be an old Coke bottle; the professor looks baffled and confesses to being utterly stumped.

Hoffenberg explains that the archeology spot resulted from his and copywriter Ted Sann's speculations on the possibility of Coke's "extinction." "Setting the commercial in the future," he continues, "allowed us to poke a little fun at the competition. Having the all-knowing professor not know what a Coke bottle was got us away from having to say something about the competition and established Pepsi as the choice of the new generation."

One of the most popular commercials in the campaign, Hoffenberg notes, is one called "Reflections." "The kids just love it," he says. "It also had some enormous production problems. Filming reflections was exceedingly difficult." Indeed, the 30-second spot is almost *all* reflections. In it, a motorcyclist speeds down a desert stretch of highway and passes a dilapidated service station. As he does so, the Pepsi logo from the station's vending machine is reflected along the chrome of his motorcycle. When the rider catches sight of the logo in his rearview mirror, he turns around and goes back for a can of Pepsi, "the spectacular taste you just can't pass up."

The campaign's most famous spot ("Michael Jackson Concert") also had some production problems. It was perhaps the most overt attempt

Archeology
60 Seconds
(SFX: Futuristic music)
Professor: This, class, is perhaps the greatest archeological discovery of our time. A dwelling called the split-level ranch. Marvelous!
Female student 1: What's this, professor?

Professor: Ah, a spherical object they used to hurl at each other with great velocity while others looked on.
Male student: What's this?
Professor: Oh . . . This device produced excruciatingly loud noises to which they would gyrate in pain.
(SFX: Laughter)
Female student 2: Professor . . .

What is it?
Professor: Odd . . .
(SFX: Whirling noise of machine removing dirt from object)
Female student 2: What is it?
Professor: I have no idea.
Anncr: VO: Pepsi. The choice of a new generation.

to present Pepsi drinkers as a part of the most contemporary of phenomena by surrounding Pepsi with all the excitement and spectacle of a Jackson rock concert. As was widely reported in the press, Jackson was burned while filming the spot when some fireworks accidently went off and set his hair ablaze. "The accident certainly heightened awareness and anticipation of the commercial," Hoffenberg observes in response to a question about any negative repercussions from the incident. "But there was no backlash. I think most people realized that it was an accident, and we all thank God that nobody was seriously hurt. It was a very fluky thing, but our crew handled the situation very well. We have the best production people in the world."

Hoffenberg had every reason to consider this phase of his Pepsi campaign a success. "Pepsi's market share rose," he says, citing a four per cent increase in sales.

Reflections
30 Seconds
(SFX: Motorcycle going full throttle. Upbeat music in background. Motorcycle slows a bit, gears shift down one gear. Motorcycle pauses, then accelerates. Engine echoes off passing building. Rock beat and surrealistic sounds. Rock beat continues, bike slows, gears shift, gravel hits metal.)
Anncr: VO: In this whole wide world, there's one spectacular taste you just can't pass up. Pepsi. The choice of a new generation.

Client: Pepsi-Cola Co.
Agency: BBDO, New York City
Art directors: Harvey Hoffenberg
("Spaceship," "Soundtruck," "Jackson
Concert," "Archeology"), George
Tweddle ("Reflections")
Copywriters: Ted Sann, Phil
Dusenberry ("Spaceship," "Soundtruck,"
"Jackson Concert," "Archeology"),
David Johnson ("Reflections")
Agency producers: Phyllis Landi
("Spaceship," "Soundtruck"), David
Frankel ("Jackson Concert"), Gene
Lofaro ("Archeology"), Nancy Perez
("Reflections")
Production companies: Fairbanks
Films, New York City ("Spaceship"),
Sunlight Productions, New York City
("Soundtruck"), Bob Giraldi Productions,
Los Angeles ("Jackson Concert"), Pytka
Productions, New York City
("Archeology"), Fairbanks Films, New
York City ("Reflections")
Directors: Ridley Scott ("Spaceship"),
Barry Meyers ("Soundtruck"), Bob
Giraldi ("Jackson Concert"), Joe Pytka
("Archeology"), Tony Scott
("Reflections")

Jackson Concert
60 Seconds
**(SFX: Jackson's music, crowd
cheers and noise)**
Jacksons (singing): You're a whole
new generation, dancin' through the day.
You're grabbin' for the magic on the run.
Anncr: VO: Pepsi presents the
Jacksons.
Jacksons (singing): A whole new
generation, you're lovin' what you do.
Put a Pepsi into motion, the choice is up
to you. Hey, hey, hey. You're the Pepsi
generation, guzzle down and taste the
thrill of today. And feel the Pepsi way.
Taste the thrill of today and feel the
Pepsi way. You're a whole new
generation. You're a whole new
generation.

Diet Pepsi

Previously cited in *Casebook 5: The Best in Advertising* for its effective use of the graphic "new wave" visual style in selling Diet Pepsi, BBDO returns with a campaign for the same client that is the "new wave"'s antithesis. Where Harvey Hoffenberg's "Now you see it now you don't" campaign relied on a hard-edged, brightly-colored, deliberately artificial look, the recent phase of the Diet Pepsi campaign uses realistic, slice-of-life vignettes that, with their soft lighting and intimate camera perspective, are warmly, emotionally engaging. Art director Don Schneider, who, along with copywriter Martha Holmes, created three of the spots presented here, observes that this intimate technique "makes viewers feel that they are in the middle of the conversation."

"It also allows the product to come up in an unobtrusive way," he continues. "Diet Coke had just burst on the scene with commercials featuring celebrities in a musical format that was like something from Radio City Music Hall. Rather than compete with that, we decided to shout with a whisper and get attention in a way that was opposite that of our competition."

This phase of the campaign also differs from the previous one in focus: the emphasis is on taste, not calorie content. Research conducted by Pepsi-Cola had revealed that the campaign's target audience, adults age 18 to 49, were less concerned with calories than they were with what Schneider calls "taste trade-off." "It seemed that taste played more of a role in the target group's selection of diet soda than diet imagery," Schneider explains. "Since Diet Pepsi began using NutraSweet [a brand of the artificial sweetener aspartame], there was less of a taste trade-off. We decided, therefore, to put less emphasis on diet-end benefit—weight loss—and more emphasis on Diet Pepsi's improved taste."

This emphasis is more or less relative, as the campaign is the ultimate in soft-sell. In one 30-second spot ("Couch"), for example, a young couple is spending a lazy, hot summer morning reading the paper and discussing their plans for the day. The mention of Diet Pepsi is almost incidental to their banter, and only comes up when the man sees that he has been drinking a diet soft drink. The point about Diet Pepsi's taste improvement is thus subtly made, and the commercial ends with the tag line, "Taste: Improved by Diet Pepsi."

In another spot ("Parking Lot"), which takes place in the parking lot of a high school, the same message is delivered, although with a younger couple. Using a similar tight camera perspective, in which only parts of the setting are revealed, the spot allows the viewer to listen in on the self-conscious courtship between a teenaged Romeo and his would-be Juliet. Again, the mention of Diet Pepsi is almost incidental to the dialog, as the courted young woman flirtatiously takes the can her suitor has been holding and tests its contents, remarking on the improved taste. The young man impatiently cites the presence of NutraSweet, and asks for a

Couch
30 Seconds
Woman: It says here that the temperature on Venus averages 800°.
Man: So let's go to the beach instead.
Woman: 29 million miles away.
Man: The beach is closer.
Woman: Here, finish this off before your ice cubes melt.
Man: Is that what I've been drinking?
Woman: Yeah, they improved it.
Man: That's one calorie? Oh, it's got that new sweetener in it.
Woman: It's sweeping the planet.
Man: Which planet?
Woman: You know, the one with the beach.
Anncr: VO: Taste. Improved by Diet Pepsi.

date. The commercial ends as he gets his ambiguous reply.

The third commercial ("Roommates") features a couple of a different sort, two college roommates getting ready for an evening with one roommate's "mystery man." Again, the intimacy of the situation is matched by the intense close-ups, and the mention of Diet Pepsi comes up as incidental to the first woman's persistent probing of just who this "mystery man" is. The subject of Diet Pepsi is dropped virtually as soon as it is mentioned, as the door bell rings and the mystery man is revealed to be the second woman's father.

A fourth Diet Pepsi commercial chosen by the *Casebook* jury departs slightly from the approach used by Holmes and Schneider. Created by art director Rich Martel and copywriter Al Merrin, the 30-second spot ("Sorority") represents an effort to re-introduce the diet "end benefit" aspect of Diet Pepsi while maintaining the emphasis on its improved taste. Slightly reminiscent of the "Roommates" spot, the commercial depicts a group of sorority sisters preparing for a date. The jingle, "Sip into something irresistible," plays on the near-pun "*Slip* into something irresistible," which is what the women are trying to do as they try on dress after dress. Again, the product is not thrust at the viewer but is portrayed as an unobtrusive, though noticeable, part of the scene. The "diet end-benefit" is demonstrated at the commercial's end by the look of awed admiration on the faces of

the three women's dates.

The campaign, which ran from 1983 through 1985, made a strong impression on its target audience despite the low-key approach. The agency reports a 15 per cent growth in Pepsi's market share as a result of the campaign, as well as "marked improvements in brand awareness and imagery ratings."

Client: Pepsi-Cola
Agency: BBDO, New York City
Art directors: Don Schneider ("Couch," "Parking Lot," "Roommates"), Al Merrin ("Sorority")
Copywriters: Martha Holmes ("Couch," "Parking Lot, "Roommates"), Al Merrin ("Sorority")
Agency producers: Ed Pollack ("Couch," "Parking Lot"), Jeff Fischgrund ("Roommates"), Gene Lofaro ("Sorority")
Production companies: Jennie and Company, London ("Couch," "Parking Lot"), Iris Films, New York City ("Roommates"), Steve Horn Productions, New York City ("Sorority")
Directors: Adrian Lyne ("Couch," Parking Lot"), Howard Guard ("Roommates"), Steve Horn ("Sorority")

Parking Lot
30 Seconds
Woman: So how come you didn't invite me?
Man: Nobody was invited, they just showed up.
Woman: Aren't you wondering why I didn't show up?
Man: Well, yeah, I was going to ask you about that.
Woman: When did you start drinking this?
Man: Since they improved it.
Woman: Hmm. Now it's got NutraSweet.
Man: Yeah.
Woman: It's good.
Man: So, uh, let's go over to Freddy's house.
Woman: Okay, but he's why I didn't show up.
Anncr: VO: Taste. Improved by Diet Pepsi.

Roommates
30 Seconds

Woman 1: So I finally get to meet him.
Woman 2: He'll be here any minute.
Woman 1: You've been keeping him a secret.
Woman 2: Oh come on . . . here, hold this.
Woman 1: Diet Pepsi does taste better than it used to. Hard to believe that's one calorie.
Woman 2: They improved it.
Woman 1: With NutraSweet.
Woman 2: Don't drink it all!
Woman 1: Are those my shoes?
Woman 2: No!
(SFX: Ding dong)
Woman 2: Here he is!
Woman 1: I'm ready. I'll probably steal him from you during dinner.
Woman 2: Not a chance. Hi, daddy!
Woman 1: Hi!

Sorority
30 Seconds

Singer: Sip into something irresistible. Sip into Diet Pepsi. Sip into something irresistible. Sip into Diet Pepsi. Put your lips to that Pepsi taste. Sip into that one calorie waist. Sip into something irresistible. Sip into Diet Pepsi.

IBM Typewriters

"IBM typewriters were already perceived by most of the market as being the best," says Gary Goldsmith, art director for this Doyle Dane Bernbach print campaign. "So we were free to sell them in an assumptive and provocative way."

The gist of the campaign is based on a "simple, universal symbol of typing that can be identified with IBM." The letterform is the essence of typing," he explains, "and it allows us to make any and every point about an IBM typewriter within the framework of a unified campaign."

Using as his main visuals enlarged, typed letterforms, Goldsmith created a campaign reminiscent of a child's alphabet primer—although with a substantially larger vocabulary. "'A' is for asynchronous communication module," one ad begins, "which is how an IBM Electronic Typewriter can become a communicating work station. Not every secretary knows that, but secretaries do know which make of typewriter they prefer. IBM." On the other end of the spectrum there is a seasonal ad printed in holiday colors of red and green. "'C' is for Christmas," it says, and suggests that business managers make a present of IBM typewriters to their offices.

Goldsmith says he encountered no problems in selling his simple idea to the client. "In fact," he recalls, "they even agreed to spend several hundred thousand more dollars to print the ads with a five-color process. This made it possible to get that brilliant, clean color, and was totally in keeping with their attitude of doing the best that can be done."

Though Goldsmith says no research was conducted to determine the campaign's effect on sales, the campaign was tested in focus groups and yielded "excellent results."

Client: IBM
Agency: Doyle Dane Bernbach, New York City
Art director: Gary Goldsmith
Copywriter: Irwin Warren
Illustrator: Gary Goldsmith

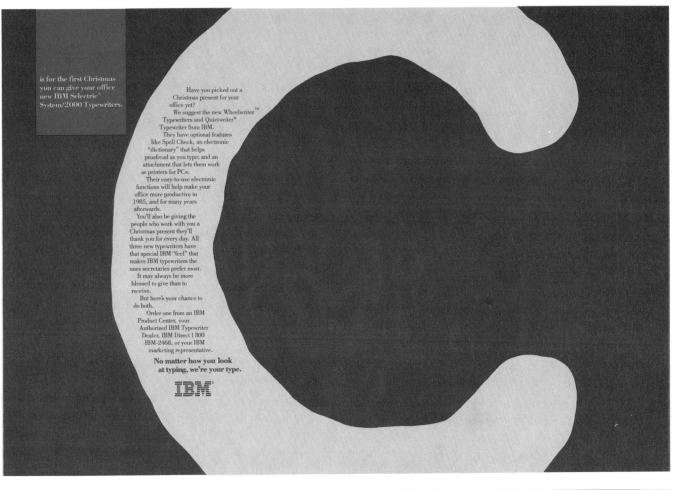

is for the first Christmas
you can give your office
new IBM Selectric®
System/2000 Typewriters.

Have you picked out a
Christmas present for your
office yet?
We suggest the new Wheelwriter™
Typewriters and Quietwriter®
Typewriter from IBM.
They have optional features
like Spell Check, an electronic
"dictionary" that helps
proofread as you type; and an
attachment that lets them work
as printers for PCs.
Their easy-to-use electronic
functions will help make your
office more productive in
1985, and for many years
afterwards.
You'll also be giving the
people who work with you a
Christmas present they'll
thank you for every day. All
three new typewriters have
that special IBM "feel" that
makes IBM typewriters the
ones secretaries prefer most.
It may always be more
blessed to give than to
receive.
But here's your chance to
do both.
Order one from an IBM
Product Center, your
Authorized IBM Typewriter
Dealer, IBM Direct 1 800
IBM-2468, or your IBM
marketing representative.

**No matter how you look
at typing, we're your type.**

IBM

is for margins
and the fact that they
adjust automatically
on an IBM
Electronic Typewriter.
"m" is also for
memory,
which along with
the ability to file,
communicate
and print,
you get with every
IBM Electronic
Typewriter.
To place an order or
get more information,
contact an
IBM Product Center,
an Authorized IBM
Typewriter Dealer
or IBM Direct
1 800 IBM-2468.
Or call your IBM
representative.

**No matter how you
look at typing, we're
your type.**

IBM

People Express

Born of a deregulated air travel industry, People Express Airline's sole marketing strategy, according to Mark Decena, art director with the airline's New York agency, Plapler Russo Wilvers and Associates, is to "offer the best value in air transportation possible." As a result, the bulk of People's print advertising consists of newspaper ads publicizing new destinations and the airline's everyday low fares.

Supplementing the newspaper campaign was a poster series that ran in New York City subways for six months of 1985. These ads, which featured full-color, realistically rendered scenes of People's vacation destinations, were aimed at the discretionary or vacation traveller living in the New York metropolitan area. "The headlines," Decena explains, "expressed People's low-price philosophy; the visual conveyed a vacation sense while merchandising People's logo."

The ad chosen by the *Casebook* jury to represent the campaign publicizes People Express's Florida resort locations with the headline, "Our vacation policy: Spend less to Florida," over a close-up illustration of the lazy doodle of a relaxed sunworshipper—the doodle, of course, being People's double-silhouette logo. "In all the subway ads," Decena says, "the problem was finding a way to make the logo stand out, but at the same time, not look too forced." Some of the other ads in the campaign, he points out, had accomplished this by depicting the logo as being made by skiers leaving a trail in the shape of the

This page: Early sketch and comp for finished ad. Opposite page: Finished ad and illustration from a small-space ad incorporating double-silhouette symbol of People Express.

OUR VACATION POLICY: SPEND LESS TO FLORIDA.

FT. MYERS·JACKSONVILLE·MELBOURNE·MIAMI·ORLANDO·ST. PETE/TAMPA·SARASOTA·WEST PALM BEACH·48 NON STOPS DAILY

PEOPLExpress
FLY SMART

silhouettes, or by forming the logo with the contrail of a passing jet. "In the original comp for this ad," he recalls, "there was just the logo drawn in the sand. Steve Schlacter, general manager for marketing with People's, points out that unlike the other ads, nothing was 'creating' the faces. He suggested that we use a crab crawling in the sand, but since we were unable to depict a crab making the silhouettes in any natural way, the human touch of the fingers was added."

Another aspect of the campaign noted by Decena is the correlation between the logo as it appears in the ads and the logo that appears on the tail of People's planes. Indeed, each ad in the campaign contains an inset photograph of the tail section on a People's airplane. "Since the logo is on the tails of the planes," Decena says, "the logo drawn in the sand reinforces the association between Florida, as represented by the beach, and People's as represented by the logo."

Decena says the ad was "well received" and was credited for a 75 per cent traffic increase to the Florida destinations.

Client: People Express Airlines
Agency: Plapler Russo Wilvers & Associates, New York City
Creative directors: Bob Phillips, John Russo
Art director: Mark Decena
Copywriter: John Russo
Illustrator: Bob Alcorn

Owens Corning
Fiberglas Pink

When Greg Sheppard, copywriter for Campbell-Ewald Canada, approached Joe Sedelmaier to do a commercial for Owens Corning's home insulation, Fiberglas Pink, his instructions were just the kind the famed director liked to hear. "The message he wanted to get across," recalls Sedelmaier executive producer Marsie Wallach, "was that if you used the product, you'd save money from lower heating bills, and just think what you could do with that money. Beyond that, he left it wide open for Joe."

Setting to work, Sedelmaier initially conceived of a spot that would consist of two vignettes of people talking about what they did with the money they saved from using Fiberglas Pink. "The first vignette was to depict a woman who used the money to buy her husband a reclining chair," Wallach recalls, "and the second was about a couple who bought enough pink, plastic flamingos to fill their yard. As Joe filmed the second vignette, he kept feeding the actors more lines. By the time the dailies were screened, it was evident that the flamingos vignette was enough for the entire commercial."

The 30-second "Flamingos" spot ran throughout Canada for a year and was so popular that Campbell-Ewald Canada president, Trevor Goodgall, contacted Sedelmaier personally to ask him to create a longer spot based on the same idea. "Joe had seen a photo of a very small house in a book by Chauncey Hare, titled *Interior America,*" Wallach recalls, "and that inspired him

Flamingos
30 Seconds
Anncr: VO: More than two million Canadians have insulated their homes with Fiberglas Pink. Here's what one particular couple did with the money they saved.
Walter: We saved enough to buy 252 beautiful pink flamingos.
Eunice: 262, Walter.
Walter: I stand corrected. Notice that all of their beaks are a beautiful shade of yellow.
Anncr: VO: What you do with the money you save is your business. Our business is making sure you do save money. Fiberglas Pink home insulation. Do it for the money you save.

to create 'Edna.'"

"Edna" is a prime example of Sedelmaier's almost surreal humor of the absurd. In it, a proud owner of a new, but tiny, vacation home, built with the money he saved from using Fiberglas Pink, shows off his new acquisition to a large number of his friends. "At the last minute," Wallach recalls, "Joe decided the house should have a name. Since many men name their boats or houses after their wives, this one became Edna."

Like its predecessor, "Edna" ran for a year throughout Canada, was extremely well-received and both spots are credited with a substantial sales increases.

Client: Owens Corning Fiberglas-Canada
Agency: Campbell-Ewald Canada, Toronto
Art director: Joe Sedelmaier
Copywriters: Greg Sheppard ("Flamingos"), Joe Sedelmaier
Agency producer: Trevor Goodgall
Production company: Sedelmaier Films, Chicago
Director: Joe Sedelmaier

Edna
60 Seconds
Anncr: VO: More than two million Canadians have insulated their homes with Fiberglas Pink Home Insulation. Here's what one particular couple did with the money they saved.
Bill: We saved enough for a down payment on what we think is one heck of a lovely summer place. As you can readily see, I named the house after my wife. Her name is Edna. And be that as it may, it gives us an opportunity to entertain our friends from different parts of the country.
Anncr: VO: What you do with the money you save is your business. Our business is making sure you do save money. Fiberglas Pink, do it for the money you save.
Guest: Bill, ol' buddy? I think I can speak for all of us in expressing our gratitude and a hearty thank you.

"Nothing is more anonymous than carpet once it's on the floor," observes Ally and Gargano art director Tom Wolsey, describing the challenge presented by his campaign for Karastan carpets. "One beige looks like another. In order to fight this, we identified with people who are 'house proud' and this led to the idea of 'nesting instincts.'"

Creative director Helayne Spivak, copywriter for the campaign, explains that Wolsey's "nesting instincts" idea was inspired by the attitudes held by the campaign's target audience of married, affluent suburban women and their husbands. "These people liked making a wonderful home for their families," she explains. "There are a lot of warm nurturing feelings in that, and that led Tom to come up with the phrase 'nesting instincts.'"

Using the theme "Some of us have more finely developed nesting instincts than others," the campaign depicts different birds "nesting" in well-appointed rooms carpeted with Karastan carpets. Wolsey explains that the ads' surreal effect was generated by using stock photos of birds placed in room models "built with an intensified perspective to work with the camera lens." "Only the carpet is real," he adds. "We wanted to create a look that would be Karastan's own," he continues. "Karastan has always had a mystique, but we wanted to enforce that and carry it further."

The ads presented here ran for a year, from February 1984 to February 1985, though account executive Martha Holland points out that the

Some of us have more finely developed nesting instincts than others.

Some of us have more finely developed nesting instincts than others.

campaign itself continued on into 1986. As for the campaign's effect on sales, she says that in 1984, when the carpet industry as a whole was enjoying a 9 per cent sales increase, Karastan could boast 28 per cent. "In early 1985," she says, "industry sales had fallen 3 per cent, but Karastan continued to grow at 5.7 per cent."

Client: Karastan
Agency: Ally and Gargano, New York City
Art director: Tom Wolsey
Copywriter: Helayne Spivak
Photographer: Henry Wolf
Rooms: Manhattan Models, New York City

Some of us have more finely developed nesting instincts than others.

INVEST IN *Karastan*

Some of us have more finely developed nesting instincts than others.

INVEST IN *Karastan*

This design breakthrough (or "burn-through," as it was hailed in the Cincinnati press) in billboard advertising was the solution to a problem presented by a casualty and property insurance agency, Frederick Rauh & Co., to Cincinnati agency James A. Jacobs, Inc.: How to get Cincinnati's business owners and corporate executives to re-examine and possibly update their companies' insurance coverage? The answer, creative director Jim Jacobs decided, was "to generate doubt in the prospects' minds about the adequacy of their present insurance coverage." "We wanted to combine a sense of doubt in the copy line with a visual representation of why people need insurance in the first place," Jacobs explains.

Jacobs and art director David Oka experimented with more conventional approaches, mainly copy lines alluding to potential catastrophe, before resorting to this unusual design which involved actually burning with blowtorches the 12, rough-cut panels that make up the billboard. "The whole thing started with punching a hole in the sign, or otherwise altering its physical conformation," Jacobs recalls. "The only problem was the necessary destruction of the billboard panels, which are normally rented by the outdoor company and reprinted or repainted from advertiser to advertiser. The outdoor company, at first, wanted to create the effect with artwork, but once the client was convinced that losing part of the message space was acceptable for the dramatic effect, the budget was

increased to accommodate the purchase of the panels."

Rotated among different locations along Cincinnati's major commuter routes over a six-month period during 1985, the billboard, with its scorched appearance and cautionary message, "Just don't *hope* you have good insurance," was a daily reminder to corporate executives driving into work from the suburbs to look into

their companies' insurance coverage. In addition to attracting the attention of local newspapers, the sign received extensive notice in the national advertising trade press. More importantly, Cincinnati's business community took notice. "At least six new accounts were opened as a result of the sign," Jacobs says. "People would drive by and get a very spooky feeling."

Opposite page and left: Comps for early proposals. Below: Finished billboard.

Client: Frederick Rauh & Co.
Agency: James A. Jacobs, Inc., Cincinnati
Art directors: Jim Jacobs, David Oka
Copywriter: Jim Jacobs
Fabricator: Norton Outdoor Advt.

Tropicana Hotel
Folies Bergere

In its effort to attract more sophisticated and affluent clientele, the Tropicana Resort and Casino in Las Vegas features a floor show named and modeled after the famous Paris revue, the Folies Bergere. "Our task," says Doyle Dane Bernbach/West art director and vice-president Jerry Gentile, "was to make people realize that the Folies Bergere is a more upscale and classy show than your typical Las Vegas revue."

Gentile's solution was a billboard campaign, an example of which is presented here, whose chief feature was soft, romantic photographs of Folies dancers taken by Deborah Turbeville. What copy there was consisted of the Tropicana logo and "Folies Bergere" written in calligraphy across the bottom of the photograph. "Without using one word," Gentile says, "we communicated that the Folies Bergere is classy, romantic, sensual and fascinating—the 'hot' show for people to see in Las Vegas."

Gentile says he got the idea for the campaign from a haunting, evocative book published by Turbeville on the palace of Versailles in Paris, in which "she had portrayed emotions and time with women." "She was the concept," Gentile says, "or, more precisely, her style was the concept. When we presented the idea to the client, we pulled images from her portfolio and used them in the comps. "We told the client, 'This is the feeling, but it won't look like this. Trust us.' Deborah had total freedom to interpret the assignment any way that moved her."

The billboards, which appeared in the Las Vegas area for six months, are credited with an 11½ per cent increase in ticket sales.

Client: Tropicana Resort and Casino
Agency: Doyle Dane Bernbach/West, Los Angeles
Art director: Jerry Gentile
Copywriter: Barbara DeSantis
Photographer: Deborah Turbeville

L'Air du Temps

According to BBDO account executive Anne Farrow, advertising for the French perfume L'Air du Temps "has a history of implied romance." "The ads would show a woman alone with her feelings," she explains, "without a male presence. Focus-group discussions revealed that though our target audience, women aged 18 to 48, liked that general approach, the romantic aspect of the message was not getting across. Our task then, was to introduce a male presence without any sexual implications, while still telling a romantic story."

Farrow recalls that art director Peggy MacNeil and copywriter Marcia Gilford, having decided on fantasy as the "best means to externalize a woman's feeling of romance," spent time "in film research and art museums" getting ideas for the look of the commercial. "We knew the feeling had to be impressionistic," she explains.

The creatives' research is evident in the gentle 30-second fantasy shown here. In it, a woman is seen musing alone in front of a painting in what appears to be an art museum. As the camera closes in on the painting, what was an impressionistically rendered scene suddenly becomes real and the woman is seen strolling peacefully within it. Not surprisingly, she meets a handsome young man and the two of them walk off hand in hand. Two doves, representing L'Air du Temps in that the stopper on a bottle of the perfume is a glass sculpture of a pair of doves, follow the woman through her fantasy while a woman's voice sings, in French,

of the "charming and enchanting dreams" inspired by L'Air du Temps. When the camera's eye returns to the museum gallery, it finds the woman gone and only a bottle of L'Air du Temps remaining.

The spot ran nationally from 1983 through 1985. Farrow says that though information regarding the spot's effect on sales is not available, post-production focus-group discussions indicated that the spot accurately conveyed the intended message that "L'Air du Temps is the most romantic fragrance a woman can wear."

Client: Jacqueline Cochran, Inc.
Agency: BBDO, New York City
Art director: Peggy MacNeil
Copywriter: Marcia Gilford
Agency producer: Jeffrey Fischgrund
Production company: Iris Films, New York City
Director: Howard Guard

Painting
30 Seconds
Woman sings: VO: *Si séduisant comme une rêve charmant rêve éveille. Né dans une reflet. L'Air du Temps c'est une vie enchantée.*
Woman: VO: L'Air du Temps, Nina Ricci, Paris. As romantic as the dreams a woman dreams.

Northlich Stolley

"This is what you expect to happen when someone sees a great ad," says Northlich Stolley art director Scott Frederick, explaining the unusual visual for his agency's house ad, "Stopper." "We were just trying to say that advertising developed by Northlich Stolley gets noticed."

The ad, which depicts an executive running flat into copy written by Northlich Stolley vice-president and creative director Craig Jackson, appeared in Cincinnati area consumer and trade magazines, as well as newspapers, throughout 1985. "We were just trying to remind clients of the importance of a creative edge," Frederick explains. "We also wanted to present Northlich Stolley as the area's most creative agency."

Frederick recalls that the agency had doubts about the ad when he and Jackson first conceived it. "We were afraid that the man's face would look disfigured," he says, "not just flattened by being stopped. We worked up some photos, and as you can see, it turned out all right."

Indeed, though Frederick says he can't "assure a business increase" as a result of running the ad, he does say the agency has received hundreds of favorable letters and comments.

Agency/client: Northlich Stolley, Cincinnati
Art director: Scott Frederick
Copywriter: Craig Jackson
Photographer: Corson Hirschfeld

When was the last time you ran into an ad you simply had to read? Chances are, it was, as we say in the trade, a "stopper." An ad with an idea so strong that it literally stops you in your tracks. An ad that not only invites readership, but demands it.

Ads like that have certain things in common. They're creative. Unusually persuasive. Maybe even a little outrageous. And, more often than not, they employ the unexpected to great advantage. But all the creativity in the world is only as good as its aim. Without it, advertising becomes nothing more than target practice. And, although practice may ultimately make perfect, what does one do in the meantime?

In your business, like ours, time is money. And the longer it takes to develop the kind of advertising that finds its mark and moves your business forward, the further you fall behind your competition. Which is something neither of us can allow to happen.

At Northlich, Stolley, we offer the talent it takes to develop highly creative advertising. And, equally important, we offer the skill it takes to keep it on target. Call 421-8840 for the kind of advertising there's just no getting around.

NORTHLICH, STOLLEY, INC.
200 West Fourth Street, Cincinnati, Ohio 45202

Pierre Cardin Licensees

This 30-second "generic dealer" spot for products bearing the Pierre Cardin designer label is a straightforward solution to what must have, at first, seemed like a problem fraught with peril. "We had to represent the interests of over 20 contributing Pierre Cardin licensees," explains BBDO account executive Anne Farrow. "And all of them demanded equal billing."

The creative team of Catherine Stern, art director, and Heni Adams, copywriter, nonetheless came up with a commercial as elegant as the clothing and accessories they were advertising. A woman, apparently preparing for a trip to France, brushes up her French by listening to a language lesson tape that, coincidently, provides the French word for each item of clothing she dons, and each piece of luggage and other accessories she gathers. These items also happen to be the products that represent the 20 or so licensees that make up BBDO's clients. "The device of the language tape allowed us to identify all the licensees' products in an unobtrusive and, more importantly, French way," Farrow observes. She points out that a similar spot was produced featuring a man.

As a "generic dealer spot," the commercial aired regionally during 1984 and 1985 in cities with retailers carrying Pierre Cardin products. The spot was offered to retailers who would obtain local air time and add their own tag line at the end. As a result, Farrow says, no information is available on the spot's effect on sales.

Client: Pierre Cardin Licensees
Agency: BBDO, New York City
Art director: Catherine Stern
Copywriter: Heni Adams
Agency producer: Gene Lofaro
Production company: HKM Associates, New York City
Director: Mike Karbelnikoff

French Lesson—Woman
30 Seconds
Male anncr: VO: *Bonjour.* The lesson begins . . . *S'il vous plait. Le peignoir. La chemisier. Les bas. Les bijoux. Le sac. La jupe. Les baggage. Le tailleur.*
Female anncr: VO: For style this international, you need but one foreign phrase. Pierre Cardin.

Wendy's

The third largest of all national hamburger restaurant chains, Wendy's suffered from a public misperception that their hamburgers were smaller than those of their competitors. "The other chains have names for their burgers like 'Whopper' and 'Big Mac,'" observes Cliff Freeman, copywriter with Dancer Fitzgerald Sample. "Though Wendy's calls theirs a 'single,' the fact is, there's more beef in Wendy's hamburgers than in the competition's—*they* just use bigger buns."

In an effort to clear up this misperception, Freeman and art director Donna Weinheim worked up a storyboard depicting a young couple buying a hamburger at "The Home of the Big Bun." After they receive an enormous bun containing a miniscule burger, the couple inquires rather politely as to the whereabouts of the beef. "We had Joe Sedelmaier in mind when we put it together," Freeman recalls. "I won't say we wrote it for him, because he hates that, but we had him in mind."

Leaving the set and dialog nearly identical to that of the original storyboard, Sedelmaier, as is his wont, changed the spot's atmosphere by replacing the storyboard's counter person and young couple with a trio of elderly women. "Joe was bothered by the fact that the young couple was so subdued and not showing any anger," explains Sedelmaier's executive producer, Marsie Wallach. "But it wasn't until two days before the shoot that he thought of using little old ladies. After all, who else would be so polite in that situation?"

In the finished version of the spot, however, one of the "little old ladies" is not so polite: Charged with uttering the inquiry as to the whereabouts of the hamburger's beef, actress Clara Peller turned what was written as a polite question into an outraged demand. As Freeman notes: "When I wrote the commercial, the focus of the comedy wasn't on the line 'Where's the beef?' It was on the ludicrously large bun and tiny hamburger. It was Clara who put the comic focus on the line; she created the phenomenon with her wonderful voice."

The phenomenon Freeman refers to is that for several

Fluffy Bun (Where's the Beef?)
30 Seconds
Customer 1: It certainly is a big bun.
Customer 2: It's a very big bun.
Customer 1: A big fluffy bun.
Customer 2: It's a very . . . big . . . fluffy . . . bun.
Customer 3: Where's the beef?
Anncr: VO: Some hamburger places give you a lot less beef on a lot of bun.
Customer 3: Where's the beef?
Anncr: VO: At Wendy's, we serve a hamburger we modestly call a Single, and Wendy's Single has more beef than the Whopper or Big Mac. At Wendy's you get more beef and less bun.
Customer 3: Hey! Where's the beef? I don't think there's anybody back there.
Anncr: VO: You want something better. You're Wendy's kind of people.

months during 1984 "Where's the beef?" became a national catch phrase. Used everywhere from high school hallways to church pulpits, the phrase reached a zenith of sorts when presidential candidate Walter Mondale picked it up for use in *his* campaign. Ironically, the line's popularity made Freeman's and Sedelmaier's job all that much more difficult. "After using it in a few more spots," Freeman recalls, "we realized that it was getting worn out—that it was becoming like verbal wallpaper. The onus on us was to keep doing commercials that were fresh and stood alone."

For that reason, Freeman and Sedelmaier decided to wrap up the "Where's the beef?" phase of their Wendy's campaign with a spot ("Road") in which Clara and two friends drive around in a 1948 Chrysler looking for the beef. As they pull up to various drive-up windows, Clara shouts her question, but is cut off by the windows being slammed shut. "I just had a mental image of Clara behind a steering wheel, driving around," Freeman recalls. "The rest was Joe's."

The third Wendy's spot presented here is from the phase of the campaign following "Where's the beef?" "Basically," Freeman explains, "what we wanted to say was that Wendy's has a lot of different choices of things to eat and the competition doesn't." To that end, Freeman worked up a script for a commercial depicting a hypothetical fashion show taking place in the Soviet Union, a country not known for its wide selection of fashionable goods available to the

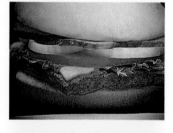

Fluffy Bun (Road)
30 Seconds
(Vamp music)
Clara: Where's the b . . . . !
Anncr: VO: At Wendy's you can drive right up and order Wendy's Single and get more beef than the Whopper or Big Mac.
Clara: Where's the b . . . . !
Anncr: VO: You want something better. You're Wendy's kind of people.

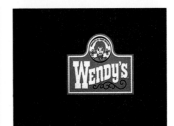

consumer. Freeman recalls reading the script over the phone to Sedelmaier, who "loved it right away."

Shot in an appropriately-decorated country club on the outskirts of Chicago, the spot ("Russian Fashion Show") depicts a fashion show in which all the different dresses modeled are the same dress. "It wasn't until we were actually on the set that Joe decided to use the same model for each sequence," Wallach recalls, "which kept the whole thing simple and stressed the choice theme. He also decided at the last minute to give the model a flashlight for the evening-wear sequence, and the subtitles weren't thought of until the final transfer to the videotape."

Freeman says that both the "Where's the beef?" and "choice" segments of the campaign were enormously successful. "Sales went up around 30 per cent after the 'Where's the beef?' campaign broke," he says. "Things weren't as clear for the 'choice' segment. We were being outspent by the competition. Still, the campaign got a lot of attention for Wendy's, and that's important. Because, when people are thinking about a place to go eat, they're more likely to go to a place being talked about."

Fashion Show
60 Seconds
(Music and applause)
Mistress of ceremonies (heavy accent): Pay attention, please. Thank you . . .
   Next . . . daywear.
(Music and applause)
MC: VO: Very nice.
   Is next . . . Eveningwear. Very nice.
Anncr: Having no choice is no fun. So everyone who wants choices is at Wendy's. Wendy's has a new light menu featuring light calorie salads, not-stuffed baked potato with many delicious toppings, six kinds of sandwiches with regular or multi-grain buns, hot chili and more. Having a choice is better than not.
(Music and applause subside)
MC: Is next . . . Swimwear.
(Music and applause)
Anncr: Wendy's. There's no better choice.

Client: Wendy's, Inc.
Agency: Dancer Fitzgerald Sample, New York City
Art director: Donna Weinheim
Copywriter: Cliff Freeman
Agency producer: Sue Scherl
Production company: Sedelmaier Films, Chicago
Director: Joe Sedelmaier

Nicolay Zurek
Photography

When art director Jerry Berman, a principal of Sidjakov, Berman & Gomez, agreed to help photographer Nicolay Zurek attract more business from art directors and designers needing location photography, he first considered a standard approach: A Zurek photograph with the photographer's name and address. "But we wanted to create an idea in addition to showing off his photography," he recalls, "knowing that a creative approach would make the ads more memorable."

The solution Berman developed couples the photographer's last name, Zurek, with different locations around the world, while at the same time showcasing one of his photographs taken at that location. "The idea came with the sudden realization of the similarity between 'Zurek' and 'Zurich,'" Berman recalls. "Then, I took it a step further and juxtaposed his name with unexpected locations, which made it memorable the way 'Paris, Texas' is memorable." Indeed, there is an ad titled Zurek, Texas, as well as Zurek, France; Zurek, Australia, and Zurek, Germany. As Zurek gets more work, the campaign expands. As this *Casebook* was being prepared, a new assignment for Zurek led to a sixth ad: Zurek, Kuwait.

Berman says the campaign, which appeared in international design magazines beginning in 1985, "has led to new assignments as well as new photography representatives in other cities for the client. The longer the campaign runs, the more interest and inquiries there seem to be."

Client: Nicolay Zurek Photography
Agency: Sidjakov Berman & Gomez, San Francisco
Art director/copywriter: Jerry Berman
Photographer: Nicolay Zurek

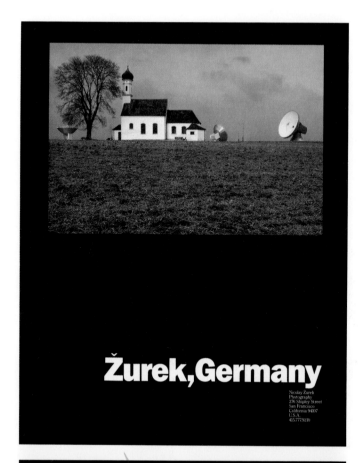

Žurek, Germany

Nicolay Zurek
Photography
276 Shipley Street
San Francisco
California 94107
U.S.A.
415.777.9210

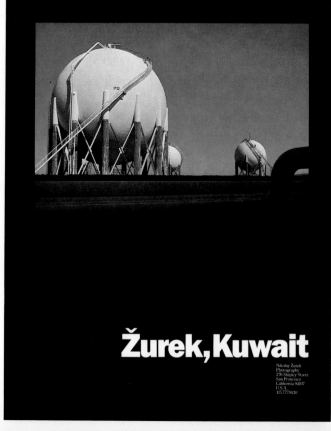

Žurek, Kuwait

Nicolay Zurek
Photography
276 Shipley Street
San Francisco
California 94107
U.S.A.
415.777.9210

Žurek, France

Nicolay Žurek
Photography
276 Shipley Street
San Francisco
California 94107
U.S.A.
415.772.9210

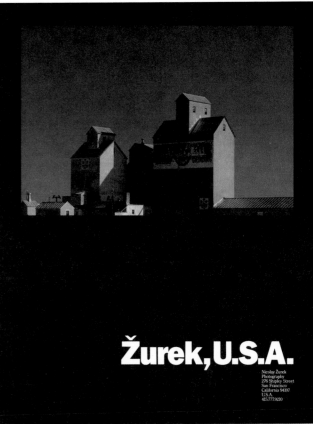

Žurek, U.S.A.

Nicolay Žurek
Photography
276 Shipley Street
San Francisco
California 94107
U.S.A.
415.772.9210

Žurek, Texas

Nikolay Žurek
Photography
276 Shipley Street
San Francisco
California 94107
U.S.A.
415.772.9210

Žurek, Australia

Nicolay Žurek
Photography
276 Shipley Street
San Francisco
California 94107
U.S.A.
415.772.9210

Davanni's

For several years, the Minneapolis agency of Fallon McElligott Rice had been creating award-winning and memorable advertising for a midwestern chain of Italian restaurants called Pontillo's. As a result of the agency's efforts, Pontillo's had one of the most recognizable names of any restaurant in the Midwest. The chain was doing well enough, in fact, that the corporate managers expanded their operations toward the East Coast, and that's when they ran into a problem: A potential competitor had a name very similar to Pontillo's, and after extensive legal negotiations, the corporation decided to change its name to Davanni's to avoid violating its competitor's trademark.

"You could hear the question 'why?, why?, why?' echoing around here for days," recalls art director Pat Burnham. "We told them to do anything but change their name, but of course they tried everything, so we were stuck with a name change."

Burnham and copywriter Jarl Olsen decided that the best way to reassure Pontillo's existing customers that though its name had changed, nothing else had, was "to make some noise and get some notice." Using a technique that is reminiscent of the agency's campaign for another local client, 7 South Eighth Street for Hair (see *Casebooks 6: The Best in Advertising*), the creatives coupled stock photos of famous personalities that are known to have changed their names with clever copylines announcing Pontillo's name change to Davanni's. For example, an ad

featuring a photo of William Claude Dukenfield, better known as W.C. Fields, notes that when Mr. Dukenfield changed his name, "he didn't part with his sauce." "We've got a new name," the ad concludes, "but we've still got the same great pizza and hot hoagies." Other ads in the campaign feature Marion Morrison (John Wayne), Karol Wojtyla (Pope John Paul II), Jayne Palmer (Jane Mansfield), William Pratt (Boris Karloff), Norma Jean Mortenson (Marilyn Monroe), and Bela Blasko (Bela Legosi). "We were doing a name change," Olsen says, "so it seemed natural to use people who had changed their names."

The campaign ran for six months in regional newspapers and consumer magazines, as well as in the form of posters. "People just loved it," Burnham says of consumers' reaction.

"Yeah," Olsen agrees wryly, "they stole the posters."

Client: Davanni's
Agency: Fallon McElligott Rice, Minneapolis
Art director: Pat Burnham
Copywriter: Jarl Olsen

When Bela Blasko changed his name, no one said it sucked.

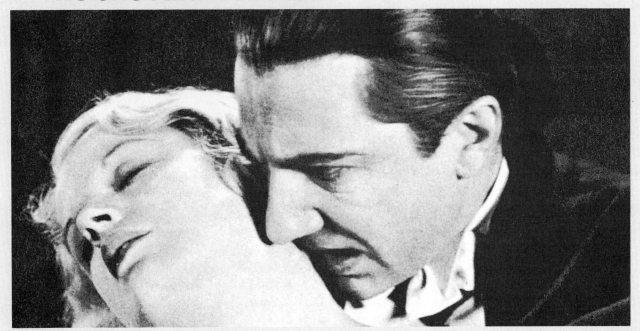

We've got a new name. But we've still got the same great pizza and hot hoagies.

FORMERLY PONTILLO'S

Acutrim

When focus groups conducted by Ally and Gargano for Ciba-Geigy's new 16-hour appetite suppressant, Acutrim, revealed that a majority of women actually resented the testimonial approach typically used in advertising for such products, it confirmed a suspicion long held by creative director Helayne Spivak, copywriter for the account. "These women felt that the skinny girls shown in the ads never had to diet in their lives," she says. "And even if the testimonials were true, they felt, 'That's her, not me.'"

Drawing upon her own experiences of dieting, as well as the findings of the focus groups, Spivak and art director Jim Handloser developed a commercial that Spivak says "let us speak to the consumer from her point of view without being condescending or phony." "We wanted the women to see themselves," she explains. "We wanted to show that Acutrim understands how easy it is to cheat on your diet when your appetite suppressant wears off and you're left to your own devices."

The 30-second spot ("Nighttime Refrigerator") humorously depicts the overwhelming temptation felt by a woman whose appetite suppressant has worn off in the middle of the night. At first, she is sitting quietly, taking care of some last-minute correspondence. Suddenly, her appetite suppressant wears off and she is literally pulled involuntarily to her refrigerator by some unseen, mysterious force. Because Acutrim is effective for 16 hours, not 12 like the other brands, the commercial concludes, "It's at its strongest when you're at your weakest."

A variety of techniques were used to create the effect of an unseen force drawing the woman to her refrigerator, the most elaborate of which, Handloser says, was a set built at an angle. "When she flew around the corner from her living room to the kitchen," he explains, "she was actually falling. But because the camera was tilted to the same angle as the set, it looked as if she were flying." For the sequence depicting the woman flying directly into the refrigerator, a standard theatrical harness was used. "We were fortunate to have an actress as athletic as she was," Handloser observes. "The harness presses on your chest and makes it hard to breathe. Most people go limp after a couple of hours, but she held up all day."

Spivak says that no sales information is available, but that the commercial was played back to focus groups, frame by frame. "The women felt that the product makers understood their dilemma," Spivak reports. "They'd sit there and say, 'Yeah, that's me!'"

Client: Ciba-Geigy
Agency: Ally and Gargano, New York City
Art director: Jim Handloser
Copywriter: Helayne Spivak
Agency producer: Mark Sitley
Production company: Power and Light Picture Co., New York City
Director: Ross Kramer

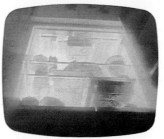

Nighttime Refrigerator
30 Seconds
Anncr: VO: It's nighttime. That 12-hour appetite suppressant you took this morning just wore off. You're all alone with your refrigerator.
(Eerie music and SFX under)

Anncr: VO: Next time, try Acutrim. Acutrim lasts longer than any other brand of appetite suppressant . . . a full 16 hours. Because you never know when temptation's going to strike. Acutrim. It's at its strongest when you're at your weakest.

Kaypro Computers

The two 30-second television commercials for Kaypro Computers shown here were designed to reach "the same small-business owner who was considering the purchase of an Apple MacIntosh or an IBM PCjr," says James Weller, co-director of creative services for Della Femina Travisano and copywriter for the campaign. "Focus-group interviews had shown us that the inexperienced small-business computer buyer believed that competitive products advertised at between $1200 and $1600 sold for $1200 and $1600 complete," he explains. "In reality, however, once software, screens and disc drives are added to those machines, the price rose to over $4000. Thus, once the consumer learned the true prices, he would buy Kaypro, which sold for $1595 complete."

Indeed, the spots as devised by Weller in collaboration with director Joe Sedelmaier, play out the situation Weller describes. In one ("Options"), a man eager to buy his first computer sits behind a keyboard, obviously pleased with the $1400 price tag. When he inquires about the missing monitor and disc drives, he is cheerfully informed by the salesmen that they are "optional." As the salesmen tally up all the computer's required "options," the dismayed customer learns that the $1400 computer actually costs $4800. The commercial ends with the voiceover: "Kaypro, the complete $1595 computer that sells for $1595."

Much the same scenario is played out in the second spot ("Complete Computer") in

Options
30 Seconds

Anncr: VO: If you're looking for a business computer, today you have a lot of options.
Customer: $1400, huh?
Salesman 1: $1400, Dick. Is it Dick? It is Dick.
Customer: Dick. Where's the monitor?
Salesman 1: That's optional.
Customer: Optional?
Salesman 2: This computer gives you a lot of options, Dick.
Salesman 1: Right you are, Bill. Optional software . . .
Salesman 2: Optional disc drives.
Salesman 1: Optional . . .
Customer: So what's this $1400 computer cost?
Salesman 1: $4800.
Customer: $4800?
Salesman 2: Right, Dick.
Anncr: VO: Some computer companies give you a lot of options. Kaypro gives you a complete computer. Kaypro. The complete $1595 computer that sells for $1595.

which another eager buyer charges into the computer store after having seen an ad for a $1200 computer. Once again, the salesman gently informs him that his $1200 computer actually sells for $5300 complete. A second salesman joins the first, and the two of them quibble about whether the $1400 computer costs $3900, or whether the $600 computer does. The customer is deflated and Kaypro's point is made.

One might be tempted to think the situations depicted in the commercials exaggerated, especially when one recalls director Joe Sedelmaier's penchant for the absurd. Weller asserts, however, that the basic *premise*, at least, of the spots is very true to life. "At first," he recalls, "*I* believed that an IBM or Apple sold for $1200 to $1600. But when I went to buy a computer, I found that they cost much more. When I took the idea to a focus group, I found that other people had had the same experience. The executions, therefore, were a direct translation of the strategy."

Weller says that although the spots ran in 1983, a period of economic recession, they were credited with a "substantial sales increase." "The economy was forcing small businesses to conserve their resources," he observes, "and being a less expensive alternative was an obvious advantage."

Client: Kaypro Computers
Agency: Della Femina Travisano, Los Angeles
Art director: Joe Sedelmaier
Copywriter/agency producer: Jim Weller
Production company: Sedelmaier Films, Chicago
Director: Joe Sedelmaier

Complete Computer
30 Seconds
Customer: Yeah, I'd like to buy this $1200 computer.
Salesman 1: That'll be $5300 complete.
Customer: $5300?
Salesman 1: What with monitor, software, disc drives . . .
Salesman 2: Etc., etc., etc.
Customer: Oh. How much is that $1000 computer?
Salesman 1: Ah, $4400.
Customer: Uh huh. How much is that $1400 computer?
Salesman 1: $3900.
Salesman 2: No, Max, the $1400 is $4800, the $600 is $3900.
Salesman 1: I thought the $1100 was $4800 and the $500 was $3900.
Salesman 2: You stand corrected.
Anncr: VO: Some computer companies give you a lot of options. Kaypro gives you a compete computer. Kaypro. The complete $1595 computer that sells for $1595.

Eurographics

Eurographics is a creative studio offering design, illustration, photography and production services to the Chicago area's ad agencies, design firms and in-house corporate design groups. "We were best-known as a production studio," says Eurographics' art director, Stefan Platzer. "But we wanted to make our clients aware of our creative talents as well."

To that end, the studio ran this full-page, four-color ad in the region's advertising and design trade magazines—such as Midwest Flash—for four months of 1985. Featuring a hauntingly beautiful photo-illustrated portrait of model Vicky Hsu, the ad attempts to graphically depict all the services offered by Eurographics. "With a name like 'Eurographics,'" Platzer says, "we wanted the ad to have a somewhat foreign style—but not too foreign, as we wanted to appeal to an American audience. We opted for imagery that grabs your attention without being clichéd—a powerful image that left room for nuance and intrigue."

The photo-illustration technique used in the ad, continues Platzer, fulfilled all those criteria with its combined "realistic and surrealistic effects." "It created something like contemporary Japanese design," he asserts, "or even something like Polish film posters. The rules, bullets and other communication tools, along with the all-American chrome lettering, showed off our talents and communicated our message." He goes on to say that he briefly considered

using a grid pattern with several designs inserted in the grid, or the same image used here set in a cityscape background, but rejected both ideas as too time-consuming and too costly to produce. "As it was," Platzer says, "the ad was done as a scanner-ready piece of art, plus a keyline for the small type, in order to save money."

The ad, according to Platzer, drew "a lot of good comments as well as a few people looking for jobs." "It's hard to say how much of a sales increase it generated," he says, "but we *are* doing more creative work now."

Client/agency: Eurographics, Chicago
Art director/copywriter/illustrator: Stefan Platzer
Photographer: François Robert

Top: Comp consisting of photograph and acetate overlay. Right: Finished ad.

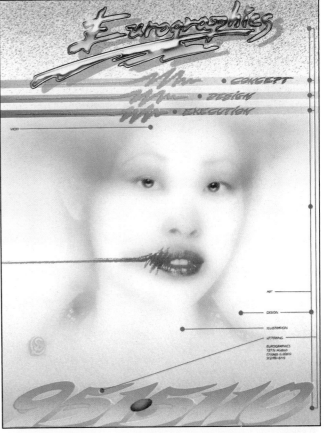

Los Angeles Olympic Organizing Committee

The circumstances surrounding the creation of these three spots for the Los Angeles Olympic Organizing Committee (LAOOC) are unusual in that the commercials represent the combined efforts of creatives who normally work for competing agencies. The occasion for this cooperative venture was the 1984 Summer Olympic Games, which were to take place in Los Angeles for the second time this century. "There was concern in the Los Angeles community that the games would disrupt the normal functioning of the city," recalls producer Jeffrey Altshuler, of Jeffrey Altshuler Productions. "And though that turned out not to be the case, the LAOOC was concerned about the prevailing public attitude."

For help in insuring public cooperation and support, the LAOOC approached the Los Angeles Advertising Club. "The Ad Club in turn," Altshuler says, "formed a committee that oversaw ten teams of creatives from different agencies in Los' Angeles." The different teams then came up with various proposals for the LAOOC. "Most of the proposals were rejected," he recalls. "This was mainly because no one was quite clear on what the LAOOC wanted. As it turned out, the LAOOC was trying to formulate its approach at the same time we were."

Finally, an approach worked out by Frank Kirk of Chiat/Day and Jim Weller of Della Femina Travisano, in which the stories of former Olympic athletes are used in appeals for support, was accepted by the LAOOC. The former athletes whose stories were to be told were

Mack Robinson
60 Seconds
Mack Robinson: VO: I was just 22 years old when we arrived in Berlin for the 1936 Olympics.

When Jessie Owens and I stepped on that track, I could feel the tension in the air.

And then, I was running faster than I'd ever run before. But that day, Jessie was a fraction of a second faster.

You know a lot of people dream of winning the Olympics, but I wouldn't trade this Silver Medal for gold.

members of a "Spirit Team," a group of Olympic athletes organized and assembled by former Olympic athlete Donna Devrona. These former Olympians agreed to volunteer their services in generating support for the Olympic Games. "Devrona also acted as the principal liaison between the LAOOC, the Ad Club committee and the production teams working on the spots," Altshuler notes. "Of all the people working on the campaign, she was the one most concerned with preserving the integrity of the athletes and the spirit and meaning of the games."

Ten members of the "Spirit Team" were chosen to have their stories recreated in 60-second spots. "All of them," says Altshuler, "were period pieces." In the spots, young actors, some of them Olympic hopefuls themselves, play the athletes as they were when they competed in the Olympics. In each case, the moment of the particular athlete's triumph, or, in one case presented here, bittersweet disappointment, is meticulously recreated.

In addition to being one of the few spots to recreate an athlete's Olympic disappointment, "Mack Robinson" is also the only spot in which the athlete himself narrates the story. Set in the Berlin Olympics of 1936, the spot follows Robinson from the moment he gets off the train at the Berlin railway station through the historic race in which he lost the 100-meter to Jesse Owens by a fraction of a second. The spot ends with the real Mack Robinson holding up the Silver Medal he won in that

Wilma Rudolph
30 Seconds
Anncr: VO: She was born the 20th child of a Tennessee farmer. Crippled by polio at the age of 4, still she dreamed of someday walking and running.

Till that historic day in Rome when she became the fastest woman in the world and Wilma Rudolph's Olympic dream came alive.

It's the same dream that will bring the fleet and the strong to Los Angeles in 1984.
Rudolph: Share the dream.

race, urging the viewer to "share the dream" and contribute to the Los Angeles Summer Olympics.

"The 60-second versions were hard-sells soliciting contributions and volunteers," Altshuler recalls. "But since we were running the spots on public-service air time, we also made 30-second versions because we thought they'd get more play. Sixties would only play as public-service late at night."

The other two spots from the campaign presented here represent those 30-second versions. One tells the story of Wilma Rudolph, who, in spite of an impoverished childhood and a bout with polio, grew up to win three Gold Medals in the Rome Olympics of 1960. The other relates the story of Pete Mehringer, who won the Gold Medal in wrestling during the Los Angeles Olympics of 1932, despite the fact that he had to teach himself the sport while growing up on a farm in Kansas. Altshuler points out that, though the low budget required all the commercials to be shot in Los Angeles and environs, the historical periods were recreated as authentically as possible. "The young actor playing Mack Robinson," he says by way of offering an example, "was wearing the exact same clothing that Robinson wore in 1936 when he got off the train in Berlin."

Altshuler also takes pains to point out that everyone connected with developing and producing the campaign donated their time. "I produced the spots at cost," he says; "the editor worked at half his normal fee, and the music was done at

Pete Mehringer
30 Seconds

Anncr: VO: It began on a farm in Kansas. A boy with a mail order course in wrestling and a dream of fame and glory. An outrageous dream.

But when the mail order wrestler won the Olympic Gold Medal in 1932, Pete Mehringer's Olympic dream came alive.

In 1984 the City of Angels becomes the Olympic City of Dreams.
Mehringer: Share the dream.

half price as well. Sidney Poitier did the voiceovers for nothing. Everyone involved got caught up in the spirit and ethic of the Olympic Games."

Client: Los Angeles Olympic Organizing Committee
Agency: Los Angeles Advertising Club
Art director: Frank Kirk
Copywriter: Jim Weller
Producer: Jeffrey Altshuler
Production company: Jeffrey Altshuler Productions, New York City
Director: Scott Lloyd-Davies

In preparation for its effort to win more advertisers, as well as more readers, for McCall's magazine, Levine Huntley Schmidt and Beaver held a series of focus-group interviews to determine what image advertisers held of the magazine. "What we discovered," says copywriter Stephanie Arnold," "was that people felt that McCall's was dated. So what we had to do, in addition to distinguishing McCall's from other women's service magazines, was to update its image."

Constrained by a small budget, Arnold, along with art directors Tana Klugherz and Tod Seisser, hit upon a campaign that featured photographs of recognizable, trend-setting celebrities who also happened to be McCall's readers. The ad copy directly challenged the notion that McCall's is old-fashioned. A photograph of rock star Tina Turner, for example, is accompanied by the copyline: "One of the drab homebodies who reads McCall's." Other ads featured Yoko Ono, Bette Midler, Carly Simon and Cher. "The idea," explains Arnold, "was to imply that McCall's was as interesting, exciting and unexpected as the readers we chose to feature in the ads."

The campaign, which began in 1984 and continued into 1985, ran in a combination of newspapers, consumer and trade magazines, and as posters throughout the New York metropolitan area. It is credited with generating an increase in ad pages for the magazine, as well as a substantial rise in newsstand sales.

Client: McCall's
Agency: Levine, Huntley, Schmidt and Beaver, New York City
Art directors: Tana Klugherz, Tod Seisser
Copywriter: Stephanie Arnold
Photographers: Scavullo (Cher, Yoko Ono), Jean Pagliuso (Carly Simon), Greg Gorman (Bette Midler), stock (Tina Turner)

ONE OF THE OLD-FASHIONED GIRLS WHO READS McCALL'S.

McCall's
MORE THAN THE EXPECTED.

ONE OF THE BORING HOUSEWIVES
WHO READS McCALL'S.

McCall's
MORE THAN THE EXPECTED.

ONE OF THE TYPICAL MOTHERS
WHO READS McCALL'S.

McCall's
MORE THAN THE EXPECTED.

ONE OF THE DRAB HOMEBODIES
WHO READS McCALL'S.

McCall's
MORE THAN THE EXPECTED.

ONE OF THE DULL CONFORMISTS
WHO READS McCALL'S.

McCall's
MORE THAN THE EXPECTED.

Alaska Airlines

The story goes that Livingston & Company's long-running campaign for Alaska Airlines, a regional air carrier serving the Far West, was inspired by a breakfast flight which John Kelly, the airline's marketing vice-president, took on a competitor airline. Expecting to be served a hot meal, he was appalled to learn that all he was getting was a doughnut. Noting that *his* airline served hot meals on every flight, he charged agency head Roger Livingston to come up with a campaign that spread the word about the differences in service between Alaska Airlines and its competition.

The resulting campaign is based on parodies of the service deficiencies of Alaska Airline's competitors. After conducting on-board surveys of frequent business flyers to determine specifically which services to parody, creative director Jerry Box and copywriter Jim Copacino devised a series of commercials that focussed on specific service problems and presented them in a problem/solution format. "We showed travellers putting up with the other airline's poor service, and contrasted that with Alaska Airlines superior, on-board service," Copacino explains.

The same approach is used in a more recent phase of the on-going campaign (art-directed by Marcus Kemp), although the emphasis here is more on problems that occur on the ground. In one spot ("Cutting Corners"), for instance, the viewer is treated to a behind-the-scenes look at how the "other" airlines choose the food they serve during their flights.

Cutting Corners
30 Seconds
Anncr: VO: These days, a lot of airlines are cutting corners on their meals.
Salesman: And this beauty we like to call banquet on a bun. Right, Bob?
Bob: Banquet on a bun.
Purchaser: I like it.
Salesman: Set it down, Bob. Now with this, you can serve a whole planeload for just pennies.
Purchaser: I like it.
Salesman: Po-lastic parsley. You can use it over and over again.
Purchaser: I like it.
Salesman: Pigmy chickens. You can get 105 in an ordinary shoe box.
Purchaser: I like it.
Anncr: VO: At Alaska Airlines, we spend a little more on our meals, and you can taste the difference.

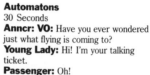

Automatons
30 Seconds

Anncr: VO: Have you ever wondered just what flying is coming to?

Young Lady: Hi! I'm your talking ticket.

Passenger: Oh!

Young Lady: Do you have baggage?

Passenger: Oh, yes!

Young Lady: Hi! I'm your talking ticket. Do you have baggage?

Passenger 2: I don't have any baggage.

Young Lady: Please enter the aircraft to the left.

Hi! Welcome aboard! Now let's adjust our seat belts. Please put your seat back in the fully upright position.

Anncr: VO: At Alaska Airlines, our people go out of their way to show you they're only human.

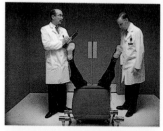

Testing
30 Seconds

Anncr: VO: Before you try anything new on Alaska Airlines, we try it first.

Tech #1: Uh, too spicy?

Tech #2: Too spicy.

Tech #3: Too spicy?

Tech #1: Uh, more?

Tech #2: More.

Tech #3: More.

Tech #1: More?

Tech #2: More.

Tech #3: More.

Tech #1: Too far.

Tech #3: Too far?

Tech #1: Too far.

Tech #3: Too far.

Tech #1: Still too spicy?

Tech #2 (choking): Still too spicy.

Tech #3: Still too spicy.

Tech #1: Louder?

Tech #2: Louder.

Tech #3: Louder.

Tech #1: Louder.

Tech #2: Louder.

Tech #3: Louder.

Tech #2: Too loud.

Tech #1: Too loud.

Tech #3: Too loud.

Anncr: VO: Why does Alaska Airlines go through all this trouble? So you won't have to.

An anonymous airline's purchasing agent sits behind a desk while salesmen show him such dubious culinary delights as "banquet-on-a-bun, plastic parsley, paté-in-a-drum," and "pigmy chickens." "I like it," the purchasing agent intones after each presentation. "At Alaska Airlines," the voiceover concludes, "we spend a little more on our meals, and you can taste the difference."

In another spot ("Testing"), the viewer gets a behind-the-scenes look of another sort: the testing department of Alaska Airlines. White-coated technicians are seen testing everything from the food to the headsets provided on Alaska Airline's flights. "Too loud?" asks one technician of another whose eyeglasses have just been shattered by the volume level on his head set. "Too loud," the second technician confirms. The concluding voiceover explains that Alaska Airlines goes through all this trouble "so you don't have to."

In a third commercial ("Automatons"), trouble begins before passengers ever get on the plane. A parody of the sometimes impersonal service provided by other airlines, the spot depicts travellers checking in at a service desk presided over by a video monitor. "Luggage?" the televised "talking ticket" asks. When the traveller answers "yes," his bag is sucked under the counter with the whoosh of a vacuum cleaner. The next passenger has no luggage, so his pants, torn off his body by the suction of the vacuum, are checked in instead. "At Alaska Airlines," the spot concludes, "our people go out of their way to show that

Bad Flight
30 Seconds
Anncr: VO: Nothing can ruin a good business trip like a bad flight. The food . . . the service . . . the crowds . . . can dull even the sharpest decision-maker.
Businessman 1: Bonnard, we've heard nothing but great things about your presentation.
Businessman 2: Raves.
Businessman 3: Fair warning: Mr. Proctor is a "show me" person.
(Chuckles from all)
Businessman 2: Break a leg, Bonnard.
Anncr: VO: Next time, try Alaska Airlines, because we do all we can do to make business trips a little easier to take.

they're only human."

In a fourth spot ("Bad Flight"), the viewer witnesses the consequences of the other airlines' poor service. A businessman, after enduring crowded airports and an abysmal flight with bad food and an uncomfortable seat, finds himself walking into an important meeting thoroughly exhausted. His prospect, he is cheerfully warned, is a "show-me person" and expects great things. Alaska Airlines, the spot concludes, does "all we can to make your business trips a little easier to take."

The final spot presented here ("Winter") is an unusual one for the campaign as it addresses a vacation, not business, traveller. It is a humorous look at the kinds of things winter-bound people will do to "put a little summer in their winters." One man tries to grill hamburgers in a blizzard, another plays golf in his living room, while a woman makes up for a solar deficiency by using a tanning parlor that roasts her like a carcass on a spit. The commercial ends with a suggestion to call Alaska Airlines "for a low-cost vacation that won't leave you cold."

The campaign, which has been running since 1982, is characterized by Copacino as "extremely successful." "Alaska Airlines continues to break all sales records," he reports.

Client: Alaska Airlines
Agency: Livingston & Co., Seattle
Art director: Marcus Kemp
Copywriter: Jim Copacino;
Steve Sandoz ("Automatons")
Agency producer: Cindy Henderson
Production company: Sedelmaier
Films, Chicago
Director: Joe Sedelmaier

Winter
30 Seconds
(SFX: Wind howling under)
Anncr: VO: The things people will do to put a little summer into their winter.
Stereo Golfer: Excellent putt, Bob. Try again.
Tanning Salesman: Oh, Mrs. Dobos, just a few more minutes. I'm putting you on spin cycle now.
Mrs. Dobos: Thank you, Carlos.
Anncr: VO: All you really have to do is ask your travel agent for an Alaska Airline California brochure. For a low-cost vacation that won't leave you cold.
(SFX: Howling wind)

Campbell's Chunky Soup

Ever since the product's introduction in the late 1970s, advertising for Campbell's Chunky Soups has been based on the successful theme, "So chunky you'll be tempted to eat it with a fork." When Campbell's wanted to increase sales of Chunky Soup among affluent, urban adults, the BBDO creative team—art director Eli Rosenthal and copywriter Gary Weintraub—decided to carry that theme over to the new commercial. "We capitalized on the same spoon and fork mnemonic that had positioned the brand for six years by taking it a step further," Weintraub explains, "while using humor to gain further interest and memorability."

The resulting 30-second spot ("Guest") is a lighthearted debate over whether a spoon or a fork is the best way to eat Campbell's Chunky Soup. In it, a man, obviously eager to impress his sexy-sounding, off-camera dinner hostess, struggles with the issue as she attempts to explain where *she* stands. When she suggests that using a fork would be manly, he picks up his fork with a bravado that is quickly deflated by her subsequent observation that a spoon is nonetheless "the proper way to eat soup." Trying to recover as quickly as possible, the hapless diner picks up his spoon with his free hand just as his hostess tells him that the quality she *really* admires in a man is decisiveness. Caught looking very indecisive, indeed, the poor fellow makes the best of his quandary by claiming to use both utensils when eating Chunky Soup. His troubles

persist, however, as the end of the meal arrives and his hostess offers him coffee or tea. Unable to decide, but not wanting to appear indecisive, he falls back on his earlier strategy: "Both," he says.

Weintraub says that although there was no problem in getting the idea to work—he notes that the commercial is "very close to the original storyboard"—he adds that he had to work under a very tight budget. "The media schedule was also limited exclusively to the 'soup season,'" he says, "which is September to February." He says the spot ran in two successive seasons, 1983/84 and 1984/85, garnering a response he characterizes as "extremely positive."

Client: Campbell Soup Co.
Agency: BBDO, New York City
Art director: Eli Rosenthal
Copywriter: Gary Weintraub
Agency producer: Michael O'Halloran
Production company: Myers Films, New York City
Director: Sid Meyers

Guest
30 Seconds
Woman: Sexy VO: I love men who eat Chunky Chicken Soup with a fork. It's so manly. Chunky's filled with chunks of chicken and noodles. You'd have to call it a meal. Of course, a spoon is so right for soup. But, what I really love is decisiveness.
Man: Uh—I always use both! Chunky's the soup that eats like a meal.
Anncr: VO: Campbell's Chunky Chicken Noodle. The soup that eats like a meal.
Woman: Sexy VO: Coffee . . . or tea?
Man: Uh, both!

Original storyboard and finished commercial.

"There really wasn't any formal marketing philosophy," designer Steven Sessions says of this small-space ad. "We just wanted the ad to be as surprising, fun and unusual as the product."

The product Sessions refers to is the "new wave" or "punk" style of haircutting offered by the Antenna Hair Salon, a Houston establishment catering to what Sessions describes as "trendy, sophisticated and daring urban young people." And, indeed, the ad is "fun and unusual" in its depiction of traditional comic strip characters "punked out" after a visit to Antenna Hair Salons.

Sessions says the main challenge posed by the ad, which, because of the client's "extremely small budget," was of necessity a small-space black-and-white, was to make it stand out on a cluttered newspaper page. "I knew comics would tend to get newspaper readers' attention," he says. "But I went a step further and floated the single frame in an area of white space. This made it look out of place and was, of course, consistent with the ad itself—I mean, who would expect 'Nancy' characters to have punk hair styles?"

Sessions says that in the three months the ad ran in Houston–area newspapers, it garnered a "very positive response." "The salon got several phone calls from new customers who had seen the ad," Sessions recalls. "And the salon attributes a sales increase of 25 per cent directly to the ad."

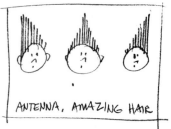

Client: Antenna Hair Salon
Agency: Steven Sessions, Inc., Houston
Art director/designer/copywriter: Steven Sessions
Illustrator: Jerry Scott

Top: Steven Sessions' "source of inspiration" and two early sketches. Above: Finished ad shown larger than actual size. Actual size of ad was 2⅞" by 2⅜".

Nike Athletic Shoes

It could fairly be said that the gist of Wieden and Kennedy's long-running campaign for Nike athletic shoes is summed up in the phrase, "Nike understands runners and running." This understanding is both in a scientific sense, as an earlier phase of the campaign highlighting Nike's extensive research and development facilities and findings demonstrated, or in an emotional sense, as the three ads chosen by the *Casebook* jurors to represent the current phase of the campaign demonstrate.

Of the three, the most obviously emotional expression of this understanding is a 30-second TV spot called "It Never Ends." Described as an "image" spot by Wieden and Kennedy account executive Kelley Stoutt, the commercial ran nationally on an intermittent basis throughout 1985 and on into 1986. In it, dawn breaks over a rural landscape and a lone man in running attire emerges from a farmhouse. After briefly limbering up on the front step, he sets off down the road at a determined pace. As he does so, the camera pulls back and skyward, revealing a beautiful vista of wheat fields, sky, and a seemingly endless road. The only sound throughout the entire spot is the runner's footsteps and the whisper of the wind. The only copy is the Nike "swoosh" logo and the brief theme line, "It never ends."

Stoutt explains that the commercial's theme line refers, first of all, to Nike's patented Airsole cushioning, which, she claims, "never breaks down." Second, the theme line refers

to Nike's commitment to runners. Third and "most importantly," she says, "'It never ends' refers to the running experience." "As long as there's a road," she explains, "the true runners will be on it."

"The idea was to show how running *feels*," she continues. "It was also to make runners understand that Nike knows what they're going through, why they run and what running means to them. That doesn't require words, it requires emotions. We wanted to capture that emotion and project it."

Stoutt says "It Never Ends" was inspired by footage shot for another Nike commercial, one to promote Nike's patented "Airsole" system. "That commercial was to talk about the power of air and how Nike had harnessed this force for running," she explains. "The runner would run through the field of wheat and the viewer would see the force of the air as it moved the wheat and turned a windmill. The storyboard called for an aerial shot of the runner, and the helicopter pilot—a Vietnam veteran who had flown in combat—did such a spectacular job of maintaining a steady, even flight path that the cameraman was able to get that beautiful continuous move that you see in the spot. It was that 30-second sequence that inspired David Kennedy, the art director, and Dan Wieden, the copywriter, to create 'It Never Ends' right there on location. Credit has to go to Nike for recognizing the idea's potential and being flexible enough to let the creatives pursue it."

The most difficult part of

It Never Ends
30 Seconds

producing "It Never Ends" had little to do with its spontaneous genesis. By the time the strategy and concept were determined, Stoutt reports, the California wheat harvest was nearing completion. Realizing that time for finding a suitable location was running out, David Kennedy asked the film crew to simply "head north" while he sought an unharvested wheat field. "They would call into the office at regular intervals to find out where they should get off Interstate Five," Stoutt recalls. "It wasn't until after they had crossed the California border that David found an unharvested wheat field in eastern Washington, giving the crew their final destination."

Though missing the statistical charts and graphs that characterized the earlier, scientific, phase of the Nike campaign, the print ad, "To Each Her Own," recalls that phase with its double-page format, compelling art and direct, matter-of-fact copy. Unlike the earlier ads, however, "To Each Her Own" delivers its message, that Nike has developed a series of lasts (the forms over which shoes are assembled) designed especially for women, in a manner that assumes a great deal of knowledge on the part of its audience. Where the previous ads sought to educate, this ad confides. "We wanted to get the idea across," Stoutt explains, "but not to be patronizing. Women athletes were breaking new ground and Nike needed to show that they understood this and were supporting women without sounding phony." Indeed, the ad's tone is respectful and frank: The copy emphasizes that although Nike thinks lasts for women are an important development, it recognizes that

TO EACH, HER OWN.

Women simply aren't created equal.
In fact, they thrive on discrimination. Give them a shoe made for a man and they'll find it too wide at the heel, too flared at the toe. But develop a model made especially for women, and they'll ask—quite properly—which woman?

Women's Odyssey

Today, runners want to know more about a shoe than what sex it was created for.
Well, at Nike, we have the largest, most technically sophisticated line of running flats ever developed for female athletes.
And finding the one that's biomechanically correct for you

Women's Terra Trainer

is pretty simple.
Every model we make falls into one of three categories: stability, lightweight cushioning or versatility.
If you need extra stability in order to control the amount of rolling around that

Women's Pegasus

occurs upon footstrike, nothing is more effective than the Women's Odyssey.
If you prefer the lighter side of running, there's the Women's Terra Trainer.
If you want a combination of both, lace up a pair of Women's Pegasus.
We make several other models as well, but they are all variations of the same three themes.
Obviously taking this approach requires a lot more research, a lot more testing. But this is one company that knows if you've seen one woman, you certainly haven't seen them all.

NIKE
Beaverton, Oregon

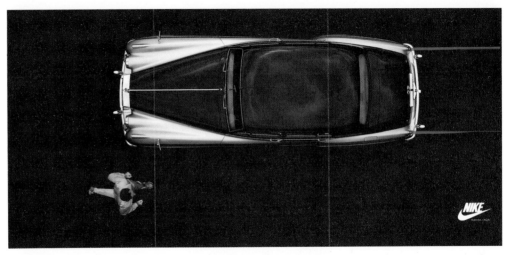

all women are not the same and promises further development. The point is emphasized with Dennis Manarchy's photograph celebrating the diversity of female feet.

Representing yet another approach to Nike advertising, one that might be considered a combination of a strictly emotional appeal and a rational argument, is the insert for Nike's top-of-the-line shoe, the Epic. "This is the best shoe Nike makes," Stoutt asserts, "and the strategy here was to promote it as Nike's Rolls Royce."

The insert is as simple as Stoutt's description. Printed on high-quality coated stock, the insert opens with the brief theme line, "Without Peers." Opening the second fold reveals a statistical breakdown worthy of any high-priced automobile, and the final fold opens a three-panel spread of an overhead shot of both a pair of Epics and a Rolls Royce in action. "This is a very high-priced product," Stoutt observes. "We were trying to reach serious, élite runners who understand the value of high quality, high performance running shoes."

Both the "To Each Her Own" and "Without Peers" ads ran in consumer magazines directed especially at runners. Though she says that Wieden and Kennedy doesn't conduct research that "directly correlates sales and advertising," she does note that both the women's line and the Epic sell "very well." "These are very good shoes," she adds modestly, "and word-of-mouth contributes to the sales."

Client: Nike, Inc.
Agency: Wieden and Kennedy, Inc., Portland, OR
Art director: David Kennedy
Copywriter: Dan Wieden

TV SEGMENT
Agency producer: David Kennedy
Production company: Riverrun Films, Hollywood
Director: Caleb Deschanel
PRINT SEGMENT
Photographers: Dennis Manarchy ("To Each Her Own"), Ancil Nance ("Without Peers")

Top right: Epic insert fully spread.
Bottom right: Last panel of Epic insert.

E   P   I   C

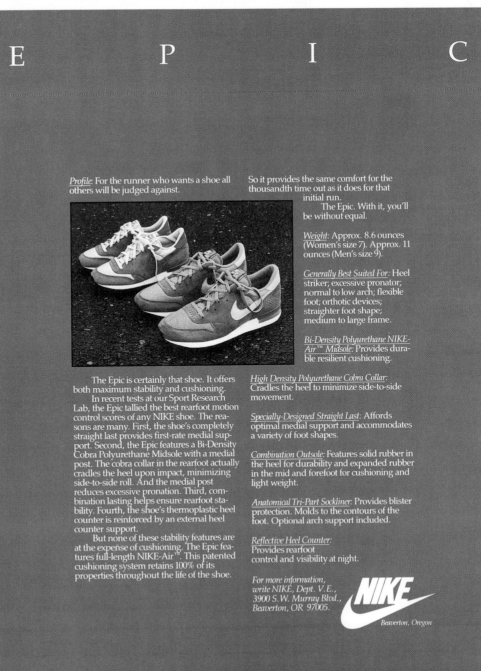

Profile: For the runner who wants a shoe all others will be judged against.

The Epic is certainly that shoe. It offers both maximum stability and cushioning.

In recent tests at our Sport Research Lab, the Epic tallied the best rearfoot motion control scores of any NIKE shoe. The reasons are many. First, the shoe's completely straight last provides first-rate medial support. Second, the Epic features a Bi-Density Cobra Polyurethane Midsole with a medial post. The cobra collar in the rearfoot actually cradles the heel upon impact, minimizing side-to-side roll. And the medial post reduces excessive pronation. Third, combination lasting helps ensure rearfoot stability. Fourth, the shoe's thermoplastic heel counter is reinforced by an external heel counter support.

But none of these stability features are at the expense of cushioning. The Epic features full-length NIKE-Air™. This patented cushioning system retains 100% of its properties throughout the life of the shoe.

So it provides the same comfort for the thousandth time out as it does for that initial run.

The Epic. With it, you'll be without equal.

Weight: Approx. 8.6 ounces (Women's size 7). Approx. 11 ounces (Men's size 9).

Generally Best Suited For: Heel striker; excessive pronator; normal to low arch; flexible foot; orthotic devices; straighter foot shape; medium to large frame.

Bi-Density Polyurethane NIKE-Air™ Midsole: Provides durable resilient cushioning.

High Density Polyurethane Cobra Collar: Cradles the heel to minimize side-to-side movement.

Specially-Designed Straight Last: Affords optimal medial support and accommodates a variety of foot shapes.

Combination Outsole: Features solid rubber in the heel for durability and expanded rubber in the mid and forefoot for cushioning and light weight.

Anatomical Tri-Part Sockliner: Provides blister protection. Molds to the contours of the foot. Optional arch support included.

Reflective Heel Counter: Provides rearfoot control and visibility at night.

For more information, write NIKE, Dept. V.E., 3900 S. W. Murray Blvd., Beaverton, OR 97005.

NIKE
Beaverton, Oregon

The elegantly simple design of the Soloflex exercise machine, which is sold through a direct-marketing program and not retailed, ironically proved to be a marketing obstacle. "The problem," Wieden and Kennedy account executive Kelly Stoutt explains, "is that the Soloflex machine looks like it only works on arm-building. We had to show that it works on other parts of the body as well."

The resulting campaign, as devised by art director David Kennedy and copywriter Dan Wieden, is as simple as the Soloflex machine itself. Running for six months in national consumer magazines, the ads each focussed on a particular set of muscles that benefitted from training on a Soloflex machine. Their rich, evocative black-and-white photography, enhanced by four-color printing, reflected a sense of quality and even elegance appropriate to the machine's somewhat premium price.

The ads, however, were intended only as teasers, for, as Stoutt points out, their objective was not to generate sales, but to "get the readers to send away for a video brochure that demonstrated how a Soloflex machine works overall." In that regard, she says, response to the campaign was "excellent."

Client: Soloflex
Agency: Wieden & Kennedy, Portland, OR
Art director: David Kennedy
Copywriter: Dan Wieden
Photographer: Dennis Manarchy

It is a symbol of heart, of courage. And to develop it properly, requires a good deal of both.

Just as essential is the right piece of equipment. Each exercise must be performed correctly. Correct in form. Correct in balance.

For if the two major muscle groups which comprise the human chest are to grow quickly, and with natural symmetry, there must be proper resistance throughout a natural range of motion.

Soloflex builds the chest. With the same efficiency and simplicity that it builds the rest of the body.

For a free brochure, call 1-800-453-9000. In Canada, 1-800-543-1005. VHS Video brochure also available upon request.

THE CHEST.

SOLOFLEX

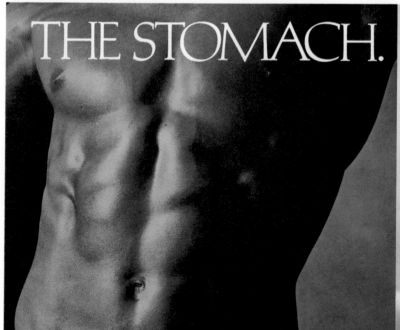

THE STOMACH.

From here, said the ancients, spring all human passions and mystical powers. Yet it is also a point of vulnerability. And how well the entire body functions, depends, in part, upon its relative strength and tone.

In the human abdomen, there are three major muscle groups. To reach them all and develop each in proper proportion, requires more than a single workout station.

Soloflex offers five. Which is why Soloflex builds the stomach. With the same efficiency and simplicity that it builds the rest of the body.

For a free brochure, call 1-800-453-9000. In Canada, 1-800-543-1005. VHS Video brochure also available upon request.

SOLOFLEX

Created in response to a shrinking market resulting from growing consumer concern with health matters, light beers have not only enabled their producers to maintain significant shares of their markets, but have widened the potential market to include more women, who, in years past, were responsible for only a small fraction of total beer consumption. Though not aimed exclusively at women, this campaign for Pabst Light, the print segment for which is presented here, is interesting as one of the first attempts to address this new and growing sector of the beer market.

Originally conceived for the existing brand, Pabst's Extra Light Beer (which contains 70 calories—"light" beer is defined as containing around 100), the campaign was inspired by target group research indicating, in the words of Young & Rubicam/ Chicago copywriter Mike Faems, "that a group of beer drinkers, women among them, was emerging that did not want a 'beer gut.'" "It occurred to us that these healthy, fit, outdoorsy beer drinkers were

giving a new definition to the term 'beer belly,'" Faems recalls. "Hence, the new 'beer belly.' We thought we'd show the best of these new beer bellies—how could anyone not pay attention?"

It was not until the idea was tested in focus groups, however, that the creatives, Faems and art director Tom Shortlidge, got the inspiration for its eventual application. "We thought fitness and health-conscious people would be very concerned about calorie content," explains Faems, "which is why we created the campaign for an extra light beer. But when we showed our ideas to a focus group, they pointed out to us that they would also be great for a regular light beer. As a result, the brewery decided to use the campaign for a new product, Pabst Light, which had a potentially larger market than the extra light beer."

Though Faems characterizes the campaign as "one of those rare ideas that sell themselves," he says the main problem with making it work was "determining what a great beer

belly looked like." "It seemed as if everyone had a different idea about how flat or muscular it should be," he recalls wryly. "But one advantage to the approach was that no faces were seen in either the print or TV ads, and that resulted in considerable savings in talent payments." Indeed, the

campaign consists simply of photographs of svelte midsections, both male and female, coupled with the headline, "This beer belly brought to you by Pabst Light."

Faems says that the campaign, which ran from March to May of 1984, and sporadically thereafter, had a

"universal appeal." "People saw it, understood it and liked it almost instantly," he claims. "It was a kick to present because people's faces would light up as they got the idea. Unfortunately," he continues, "the brewery was acquired by new owners early in 1985 and they immediately dropped all

advertising for Pabst brands. We feel that if the campaign had been allowed to run its course, it could have become a classic."

Client: Pabst Brewing
Agency: Young & Rubicam, Chicago
Art director: Tom Shortlidge
Copywriter: Mike Faems
Photographer: JoAnn Carney

AMF Heavy Hands

This campaign for AMF Heavy Hands—exercise aids used to increase the benefit derived from an existing exercise program—is actually two campaigns. Fallon McElligott Rice account executive Peter Engel explains that the campaign's dual approach was based on several industry studies on the exercise market. "These studies," he says, "dealt with why people exercise as well as what kinds of exercise they preferred. They indicated that the exercise market actually consists of two groups: people already participating in some form of exercise, and individuals who have not yet begun an exercise program." While the studies indicated that both groups were concerned with fitness, it seemed that they each had their own definition of what fitness was. "For the first group," Engel explains, "fitness meant 'wellness'; weight loss was a secondary issue with them. In the second group, however, fitness meant 'weight loss,' not wellness. These people had tried various exercise programs in the past, but had to abandon them because of poor results."

Though all the ads in the campaign deliver the same message and are consistent with one another visually in that they all employ a split visual format, individual ads are tailored to address one of the two main consumer groups. The ad "See Dick run . . . ," for instance, features a man running alongside a woman running with Heavy Hands. The copy points out that by using Heavy Hands, "Jane" is burning 30 per cent more calories than "Dick." Another ad features a

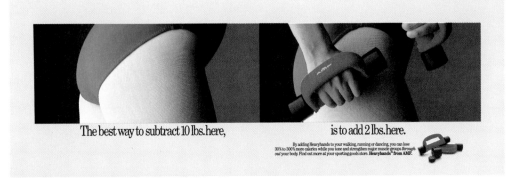

The best way to subtract 10 lbs. here,
is to add 2 lbs. here.

By adding Heavyhands to your walking, running or dancing, you can lose 30% to 300% more calories while you tone and strengthen major muscle groups *throughout* your body. Find out more at your sporting goods store. **Heavyhands™ from AMF.**

See Dick run.
See Jane run.

See Jane burn 30% more calories.

Tests prove that running with Heavyhands not only increases aerobic capacity, but also burns between 30% and 100% more calories than running without Heavyhands.

At the same time, Heavyhands help tone and strengthen major muscle groups *throughout* the body, while decreasing the danger of injury.

Find out why more and more serious runners everywhere are using Heavyhands at your local running store. **Heavyhands™ from AMF.**

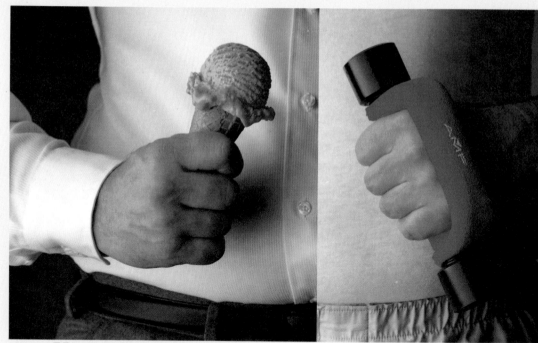

You put it on with your hands,   now take it off with your hands.

By adding Heavyhands to your walking, running or dancing, you can lose 30% to 300% more calories while you tone and strengthen major muscle groups *throughout* your body. Find out more at your sporting goods store. **Heavyhands™ from AMF.**

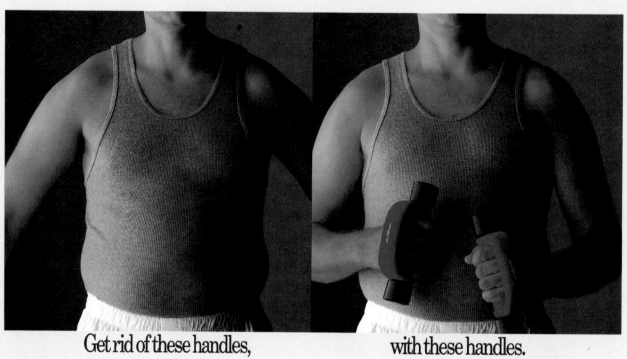

Get rid of these handles,   with these handles.

By adding Heavyhands to your walking, running or dancing, you can lose 30% to 300% more calories while you tone and strengthen major muscle groups *throughout* your body. Find out more at your local sporting goods store. **Heavyhands™ from AMF.**

woman doing aerobic dancing, first without Heavy Hands, then with. The copylines tell the whole story: Over the picture of her dancing without the weights, it reads, "Dance, dance, dance . . . lose, lose, lose." Over the picture of her dancing with Heavy Hands, it reads, "Dance, dance, dance . . . lose, lose, lose, lose, lose, lose," illustrating the advantage of using Heavy Hands in both a visual and verbal way. "The copy emphasizes that with Heavy Hands, one burns calories faster," Engel says. "And that translates into a better workout. We used running and aerobic dancing as examples because both sports are popular among today's fitness consumers, and people using these exercises want the maximum benefit from their workouts."

Though the body copy is almost identical to that of the others, the ads directed at the second group of consumers, i.e., those interested in losing weight, use the split visual format for a before and after picture of another sort. Using a problem/solution format, the ads translate the increased expenditure of calories provided by Heavy Hands into faster weight loss. One spread, featuring a somewhat chubby male torso, suggests that the unsightly bulges euphemistically referred to as "love handles," are quickly removed by using "these handles": Heavy Hands. Another ad featuring the same overweight physique clutching an ice cream cone, points out that "you put it on with your hands," and suggests that with an exercise program using

Heavy Hands, "you can take it off with your hands." The third ad in that group is directed at women and points out that to "subtract ten pounds here (in the hips and thighs)," you "add two pounds here (in the hands with Heavy Hands)." "The combination of provocative headlines and dramatic photographs communicate that you can lose weight faster with Heavy Hands," Engel concludes.

The campaign ran for a year in consumer magazines nationwide and is credited by the client, Engel says, with generating a substantial sales increase.

Client: AMF American
Agency: Fallon McElligott Rice, Minneapolis
Art director: John Morrison
Copywriter: Tom McElligott
Photographer: Dennis Manarchy

Dance, dance, dance.

Lose, lose, lose.

Dance, dance, dance.

Lose, lose, lose, lose, lose, lose, lose, lose, lose.

Aerobic dancing with Heavyhands burns 30% to 100% more calories than aerobic dancing without Heavyhands.
At the same time, Heavyhands help tone and strengthen major muscle groups *throughout* the body while promoting unparalleled aerobic efficiency.
Find out why more and more serious exercisers are dancing with Heavyhands at your local sporting goods dealer.

Heavyhands from AMF.

When a free placement service for handicapped workers was being formed in Minneapolis, its organizers approached Fallon McElligott Rice for help in publicizing their services and coming up with a name for those services. "That was probably the hardest part," says copywriter Jarl Olsen. "We wanted a name that dwelled on these people's abilities, not disabilities. We finally settled on 'Hire Ability.'"

The tone of the year-long print campaign thus set, Olsen, along with art director John Morrison, created a series of inexpensive yet powerful ads that used a combination of cleverly utilized stock photography and sharp, sometimes (daringly) waggish copy. One ad, for example, features a photograph of a wheelchair-borne woman smiling at what is obviously her college graduation exercise. The copy encourages the reader to "hire her, she's got great arms." "The idea was to 'sell' persons with disabilities as qualified, responsible workers," Olsen says. "We also included some ads that were run just to heighten the public's awareness of the handicapped worker. We used examples of people who had no trouble working with their disabilities." One such ad, Olsen says, consists of a photo of a grinning Franklin Roosevelt, who was crippled from polio throughout his presidency, over the copyline, "Hire the handicapped, your parents did." More recent examples of able handicapped achievers are featured in other ads, among them musician Ray Charles and president Ronald Reagan (who are blind and hearing-impaired, respectively).

Olsen says that reaction to the campaign, which ran in Minneapolis area trade and consumer magazines, as well as newspapers, through 1984, was mixed. "Some people found the ads tasteless," he reports. "But the people with the disabilities weren't so easily offended."

Client: Hire Ability
Agency: Fallon McElligott Rice, Minneapolis
Art director/designer: John Morrison
Copywriter: Jarl Olsen

Hire the handicapped.
Your parents did.

Hiring someone on their merits isn't a new idea. Just a good one. Call us when you need someone who can get the job done.

HIRE ABILITY
800-828-9095

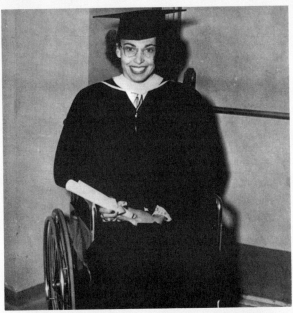

Hire her. She's got great arms.

Please, the next time you look at someone with a disability, think of what they *can* do.

Call us and see if we don't have someone who is everything you need.

HIRE ABILITY
800-229-9086

What kind of job can you give someone with a disability?

President Reagan has a hearing loss. President Kennedy had a spinal injury. President Roosevelt had polio.

Now, what was it you wanted to know about hiring someone with a disability?

HIRE ABILITY
800-229-9086

There have always been career opportunities for the disabled.

It's time people with disabilities got some new jobs to pick from. If you have a position open, please call us. We have applicants who can do almost everything.

HIRE ABILITY
800-229-9086

What do you do if you're disabled and you don't sing or play the piano?

People with disabilities have talents you probably never realized.

We know. We place them everyday in businesses just like yours.

HIRE ABILITY
800-229-9086

18th and Vine
Historic Jazz
District Museum

This ad, donated as a public service by John Muller & Co., was, in the words of agency president John Muller, "to remind the public of Kansas City's jazz heritage and to garner public support for the 18th and Vine Historic Jazz District Museum, which was just beginning to undergo development." Because of the museum's limited advertising budget, the ad ran only once in Kansas City newspapers. "For that reason," Muller says, "we knew we had to produce a very simple, high-impact ad that would elicit a lot of emotion and a big response."

Still, Muller recalls the inspiration and conception of the ad as being practically instantaneous. "I was doing some research for a poster for the same client," he recalls, "when I came across a wonderful old photograph of Eddie 'Cleanhead' Vinson. I said to myself, almost unconsciously, 'Wow! Just look at him wailing away!' The ad just evolved from there. The whole conception took about ten minutes. We went straight from the rough to the mechanical."

Indeed, the process Muller describes is well documented in his original layout, which, true to the spontaneous nature of its conception, is scrawled on the back of a manila envelope. The ad's headline, a play on the old environmentalist rallying cry, clearly evolved from Muller's first impression of the old photo that makes up the ad's visual.

Muller says that despite the ad's brief public appearance, he has received "hundreds of comments and requests for reprints."

Client: Kansas City Jazz Commission/ Kansas City Star
Agency: John Muller & Co., Kansas City, MO
Art director/copywriter: John Muller

Support the Development of the National Jazz Museum in Kansas City's 18th & Vine Historic District.

In the never-ending ratings struggle among radio stations on the New York metropolitan area's AM dial, one station, WNEW 1130, has for years held steady with its programming of popular music from the '40s and '50s. An oasis of light jazz ballads on the rock-and-news-jammed airwaves, WNEW consistently attracted an affluent audience of adults 35 and older. In 1985, fearing that the format was growing a little stale, the station management decided to tighten up the playlist to include more recordings by the most popular performers, and to include broadcasts of live performances.

Concurrent with the programming change was a new ad campaign by New York's Holland & Calloway. The station's previous advertising, created by another agency, had emphasized the nostalgic aspect of the music with the bittersweet theme, "Where the melody lingers on." "Our attack," says Les Bridges, copywriter with Holland & Calloway, "was to focus on the epic quality of the performers and the music, as well as to present that point of view with a technique as contemporary as MTV."

Based on preferences expressed in listener requests and focus-group interviews, Bridges, creative director Ron Holland, and illustrator Bob Hickson devised a poster campaign featuring airbrushed portraits of the most popular performers of '40s and '50s era pop music. Rendered in electric pastel colors, the posters have a proud, aggressive tone which is verbally expressed by the theme line, "Blessed with

America's Best." Bridges recalls the inspiration for the campaign as being the colorful images projected by the stars of more contemporary popular music. "I remember seeing Van Halen on MTV," he explains, "and realizing that Louis Armstrong and Ella Fitzgerald would have just as much energy if presented in a contemporary way. Hence, the California airbrush and the 'Miami Vice' colors." ("Miami Vice" is the popular television police series set in Miama, Florida, that, among other things, features a trend-setting palette of tropical colors.)

The posters, two of which were selected by the *Casebook* jurors, appeared in bus, train and subway stations throughout the New York metropolitan area during most of 1985, and proved to be highly popular— almost to the detriment of the campaign. "Several thousand posters were stolen from the subways," Bridges explains. "And a two-month showing in bus shelters was shortened to two weeks when those posters were swiped." Nonetheless, an independent auditing group, Arbitron, posted an audience increase for WNEW of 24 per cent, which the station attributes directly to the poster campaign. None of this surprises Bridges, who says confidently, "We knew this was a bull's-eye from day one."

Client: Metromedia Radio, WNEW-AM
Agency: Holland & Calloway,
New York City
Creative director: Ron Holland
Art director/illustrator: Bob Hickson
Copywriters: Ron Holland,
Les Bridges

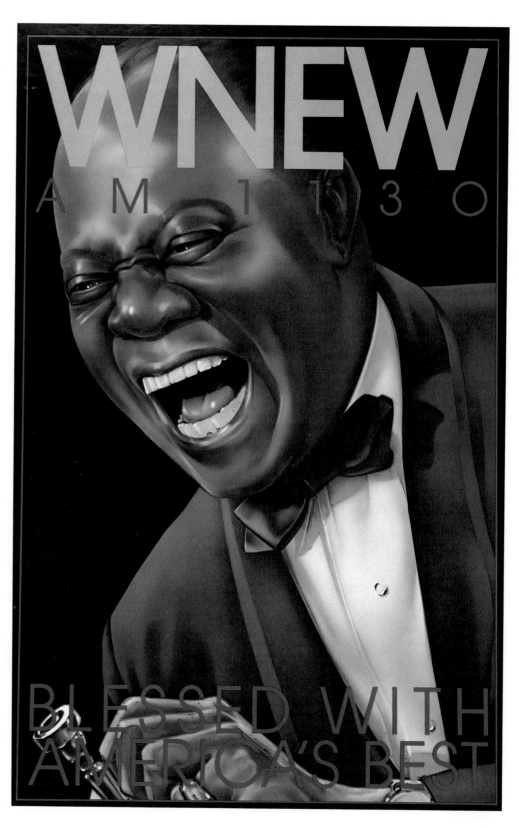

3M Commercial Office Supply Division

As Kimberly-Clark, the manufacturers of Kleenex, and the Xerox Corporation know, being the first or the finest with an important product or service is a mixed blessing. The trademarked name of your product is on everyone's lips, but people dilute the effectiveness of that trademark by turning it into a generic term. Both Xerox and Kimberly-Clark spend a significant amount of their advertising dollars fighting this "generification" of their trademarks, and though 3M is just as concerned about the problem, it has—with one ad at least—turned the practice to its advantage.

Running throughout 1985 in trade magazines nationwide, the ad was directed at 3M supply dealers whose loyalty was about to be tested by competitors entering the market with products identical or similar to those produced by 3M. "We wanted to remind those dealers of 3M's leadership and quality," says Emily Scott, copywriter with Minneapolis's Martin/Williams agency. "So we decided that good old Scotch tape would serve as the hero product to convey the marketing philosophy. We simply reminded our dealers that the name Scotch tape is at the top of everyone's mind—the dealer as well as his customers. It's the only brand that anyone can think of."

The ad, a double-page spread, presents the reader with a typical problem for anyone who works regularly with paper: An important piece of work has been torn. The headline asks, "Quick! What do you reach for?" The body copy answers, "Scotch brand tape." Scott says that she would have preferred the ad to read simply "Scotch tape," but the client was reluctant to waive copyright rules, even in this instance. She goes on to say that the ad's startling 3D effect was produced by silk-screening the headline and bottom rule directly on the background paper.

Scott characterizes the ad as a success. "In spite of increasing competition," she says, "3M has maintained its market share. So we feel it did its job. And so does 3M."

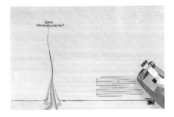

Above: Comp used for client presentation. Below: Finished ad.

Client: 3M Commercial Office Supply Div.
Agency: Martin/Williams Advertising, Minneapolis
Art director: Sally Wagner
Copywriter: Emily Scott
Photographer: Kent Severson

Norfolk General Hospital

Despite the fact that it has an excellent reputation in the international medical community, Norfolk General Hospital in Norfolk, Virginia, found its share of the Tidewater area's healthcare market eroding under intense competition from local suburban hospitals more convenient to Norfolk General's primary market of affluent suburban families. Exacerbating the problem was the fact that area healthcare consumers were generally unaware of Norfolk General's reputation, as well as the fact that these consumers were also the targets of a barrage of aggressive marketing and advertising campaigns being waged by the other hospitals. "Our research showed that most consumers in the Tidewater area made no distinction between Norfolk General and those other hospitals," explains Ken Hines, copywriter with Norfolk's Lawler Ballard Advertising. "They were unaware of the benefit of having even the most routine procedure done at a medical center of Norfolk General's caliber."

Hired by Norfolk General to reverse this trend, Hines, along with art director Don Harbor and designer Jeff France, devised a campaign to educate area residents to Norfolk General's special services and programs. The result was a series of newspaper ads that highlighted those aspects of the hospital's services that would be of interest to Norfolk General's target audience of affluent professionals and their families. The ad from that campaign shown here, for example, highlights Norfolk General's reconstructive surgery and physical therapy programs. "We knew our target audience was, for the most part, college-educated, readers rather than TV-watchers, and were the sort of people who wanted to make informed decisions about their healthcare," Hines says. "We also wanted to appeal to the natural curiosity people have about their bodies." Hines further notes that the ad's proud tone was inspired by the "intense commitment" he detected in Norfolk General's staff. "It came through unmistakably in the interviews we held," he recalls.

The campaign, by any definition, was an unqualified success: A month before it broke, calls to the hospital's physician referral line numbered only in the low 40s. Five months after it broke, such calls numbered over 350. "Readers actually called the hospital for copies of the ads," Hines recalls. "Department heads have asked for reprints of the ads to frame for their offices, and they seem to have instilled even greater pride in the nursing and support staffs."

Client: Norfolk General Hospital
Agency: Lawler Ballard Advertising, Norfolk, VA
Art director: Don Harbor
Designer: Jeff France
Copywriter: Ken Hines
Photographer: Jamie Cook
Type director: Don Woodlan

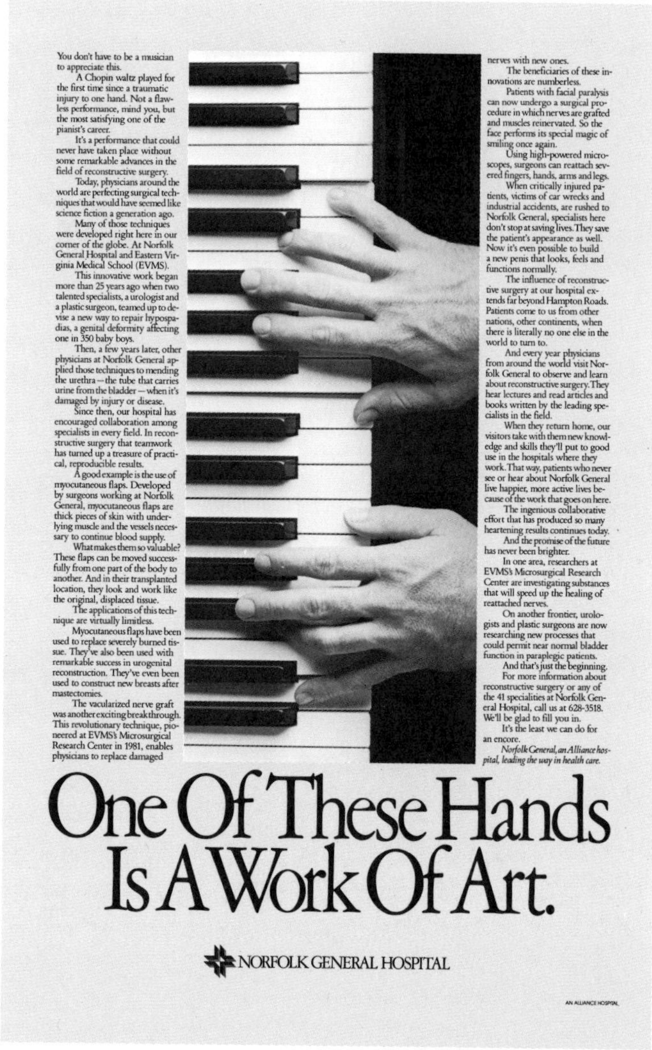

One Of These Hands Is A Work Of Art.

✦ NORFOLK GENERAL HOSPITAL

AN ALLIANCE HOSPITAL

Washburn Child Guidance

The Washburn Child Guidance Center is a Minneapolis clinic funded by private contributions to help children with learning disabilities cope with their handicaps. "The kids these people help," says Dean Hanson, Fallon McElligott Rice art director, "are the ones who gradually fall behind because of their learning disabilities."

Created to attract contributions to the center, this 60-second spot conceived by Hanson and copywriter Phil Hanft is a poignant dramatization of the phrase "falling behind." Set to the melancholy melody of Beethoven's "Moonlight Sonata," the slow-motion commercial shows a young boy running enthusiastically down a road toward the camera. As the camera pulls ahead, the boy strives to keep up, but the camera continues to pull away. Just as the boy is about to disappear into the distance, the viewer sees him give up in despair and stand forlornly in a desolate and lonely landscape. The voiceover urges the viewer to support the Washburn Child Guidance Center, "where no child is left behind."

Hanson points out that because of the commercial's slim production budget, the footage was shot with normal color film at normal speed and was slowed down in the film-to-video transfer. The spot's muted color palette, too, was created in the transfer. "The original footage was gorgeous," Hanson says. "We shot on a very sunny day, so we had a lot of saturated color. But we wanted to create a serious mood, so we toned the color down. Black-and-white signals to people that you're not jokin' around," he explains. "But since we didn't want to be entirely grim, we left that touch of color in."

The commercial began running on donated airtime in the spring of 1985 and through to 1986. Hanson says that though he is unaware of the spot's specific effect on contributions to the center, "word-of-mouth has been very positive."

Client: Washburn Child Guidance Center
Agency: Fallon McElligott Rice, Minneapolis
Art director: Dean Hanson
Copywriter: Phil Hanft
Agency producer: Judy Carter
Production company: James Gang, Dallas
Director: Jim Beresford

Washburn Child Guidance Center
60 Seconds
(SFX: Beethoven's "Moonlight Sonata")
Anncr: VO: Without special help, kids with learning and behavioral disorders can fall so far behind, they never catch up. Support the Washburn Child Guidance Center. Here, no child is left behind.

When, in the spring of 1983, a bill was introduced to the Minnesota Legislature that threatened to raise personal income and other taxes in the state, a group of Minnesota companies organized to oppose the new taxes. Political polls conducted around the state had revealed that most Minnesota taxpayers (who were already among the most heavily-taxed in the country) were unaware of the implications of the bill, so the companies, calling themselves the Minnesota Business Partnership, approached Fallon McElligott Rice for help in spreading the word about, and generating opposition to, the imminent tax hike.

"The fact that people were unaware of the potential tax increase inspired Jarl Olsen to come up with the phrase, 'taking candy from a baby,'" recalls art director Dean Hanson. "It wasn't very long before we translated that phrase into a commercial."

The resulting 30-second commercial ("Cry Baby") is, indeed, about taking candy from a baby. In it, a baby representing the Minnesota taxpayers, is shown sitting happily holding two fistfuls of candy. As its attention wanders, an adult gently takes one handful of candy away from the baby. Although a little surprised by the disappearance of some of the candy, the baby nonetheless seems content with what is left. Then, another adult hand enters the picture from the other side and takes the remaining handful of candy. The baby, candyless and confused, bursts into tears. The voiceover urges the viewer to call or write his legislator and voice his opposition to a tax increase. "Let's hang on to what we have left," it warns.

Hanson says the chief difficulty in executing the spot was "the low budget and the fact that we were working with babies." "Working with babies is risky," he explains. "We had to shoot 15 infants before we got the reaction we wanted, and shooting that many babies would have meant using a huge amount of film. As a result, we shot the spot right onto videotape in order to save money."

Hanson says the spot accomplished its purpose in that it brought the issue of new taxes "out into the open and before the public." "There was a lot of debate," he recalls. "And the bill was eventually withdrawn and reworked. We've still got one of the higher tax rates in the country, but we're not right up there on top the way we used to be."

Client: Minnesota Business Partnership
Agency: Fallon McElligott Rice, Minneapolis
Art director: Dean Hanson
Copywriter: Jarl Olsen
Agency producer: Judy Carter
Production company: James Productions, Minneapolis
Director: Jim Lund

Cry Baby
30 Seconds
(Music: Brahm's "Lullaby")
Anncr: VO: Raising taxes in Minnesota used to be like taking candy from a baby. But lately, some of our state lawmakers have had to resort to tricks. Right now, hidden in a bigger tax bill are provisions that spell permanent income tax hikes for most Minnesota taxpayers. They think we won't notice a little increase of 20 to 30 per cent. Who do they think we are—children? Call or write your legislator and tell him to hold the line. Let's hang on to what we've got left.

Stroh's Beer

A regional midwestern beer until it was marketed nationally in 1984, Stroh's had advertising that, according to Marschalk art director Gary Ennis, "would use any situation for humor." "When you're a regional beer," he says, "you can take chances like that. When Stroh's went national, however, we decided to keep the humorous approach, but keep it within typically beer-drinking situations. Beer drinkers were laughing at the old campaign, but they really couldn't relate to its bizarre situations."

Examples of typically beer-drinking situations, Ennis says, are poker games, sporting events and camping trips. "We were trying to get beer drinkers to think of Stroh's as a premium beer," Ennis explains, "and to do that we had to present Stroh's drinkers as male, macho, beer-drinking types." The spot shown here ("Alex") is one of the first created by the agency using the new emphasis.

Written by Seth Warner, the spot depicts a group of youngish men sitting around a table playing poker. When one of the players gets up to get himself a cold beer, his host tells him to sit down. "Watch this," the host says to his guests. Calling to his dog, Alex, the host instructs the pooch to bring two cold Stroh's to the table. The dog barks in assent and trots off into the kitchen, from where we hear the light switch click and see the light go on. Guided by the narration of Alex's master, we hear Alex open the refrigerator, take out the beer, open the bottles and pour the beer into glasses. When we hear the sound of a

dog drinking, it is the master's turn to bark. "Alex!" he calls sternly, "you'd better be drinking your water!"

Marschalk account executive Paul Norwhich points out that though the spot is "slightly unbelievable," it does stay within the confines of a beer-drinking situation. "As long as you stay within the bounds of that kind of situation," he says, "you're allowed a certain license."

The approach apparently worked, for as Norwhich points out, Stroh's easily met its first year's sales goals as a national brand. "But more importantly," he says, "'Alex' got more people aware of the fact that Stroh's is a premium beer—in spite of the fact that the competition was outspending us three to one."

Client: The Stroh Brewery
Agency: The Marschalk Co., Inc., New York City
Art director: Gary Ennis
Copywriter: Seth Warner
Agency producer: Paula Dwoskin
Production company: Levine Pytka, New York City
Director: Rick Levine

Alex
30 Seconds
Poker Player: I'd sure like another Stroh's.
Host: No, wait. Alex!
Dog: Arf.
Host: Two cold Stroh's.
Dog: Arf.
Host: Wait till you see this.
(SFX: Refrigerator door opening)
Host: He just opened the refrigerator.
(SFX: Bottle opening)
Host: He just opened one bottle.
(SFX: Bottle opening)
Host: He just opened the other.
(SFX: Beer being poured into glass)
Host: Now he's pouring yours.
(SFX: Other beer being poured)
Host: Now he's pouring mine.
(SFX: Dog drinking)
Host: Alex, you'd better be drinking your water!

From one beer lover to another.

Minnesota Federal

Minnesota Federal, says Fallon McElligott Rice art director Dean Hanson, aside from wanting more people to "come in and apply for loans," had a name recognition problem. "Minnesota Federal is a small bank that is somewhat overshadowed by a much larger bank, Midwest Federal," Hanson explains. "The fact that their names are similar wasn't helping much, either."

FMR's campaign, therefore, in addition to getting people into the bank, was designed to gain Minnesota Federal some "notoriety." "We decided to play on the contradiction and insincerity of typical bank advertising," Hanson says. "We were particularly goaded by another local bank's campaign which was saying 'We're on your side.' They made themselves sound so warm and friendly, but of course, when you go in there, they're businessmen like everybody else. We thought that by making fun of that kind of advertising, we'd get Minnesota Federal some notice and, hopefully, make the bank seem more accessible."

The campaign devised by Hanson, creative director Tom McElligott and copywriter Mike Lescarbeau depicts stereotypically buttoned-down and humorless bankers lip-synching to songs that reveal their true attitudes toward giving out loans. The first spot in the campaign, Hanson says, was inspired by a song from the film classic *Bringing Up Baby,* "I Can't Give You Anything But Love." "That's the impression conventional bank advertising gives you," Hanson observes. "They come across as such nice guys, but when you go in, they can't do a thing for you."

From there, the campaign picks up on two rock and roll standards: "Keep on Knockin'," and "Hit the Road Jack." Hanson says that "Keep on Knockin'," whose chorus goes "Keep on knockin' but you can't come in," is what people feel like "when they apply again and again for loans, but are always turned down." "'Hit the Road Jack,'" he continues, "is the nightmare of anyone who has ever applied for a loan. Not only are you afraid that they won't lend you the money, but also that they'll publicly humiliate you by throwing you bodily into the street."

Hanson says that the two 30-second spots were shown throughout the Minneapolis area for two years and are credited with generating an "increase in loan rates throughout the market area."

Client: Minnesota Federal
Agency: Fallon McElligott Rice, Minneapolis
Art director: Dean Hanson
Copywriters: Tom McElligott, Mike Lescarbeau
Agency producer: Judy Carter
Production companies: N. Lee Lacy, New York City ("Anything but Love"), Rossetti Films, New York City ("Hit the Road Jack"), Steigman Productions, New York ("Keep on Knockin'")
Directors: N. Lee Lacy ("Anything but Love"), Dominic Rossetti ("Hit the Road Jack"), Steve Steigman ("Keep on Knockin'")

Anything But Love
30 Seconds
Anncr: VO: For years, banks and savings and loans have been singing the same old song.
Banker 1 (singing): I can't give you anything but love, baby.
Banker 2: That's the one thing I've got plenty of, baby.
Anncr: VO: They tell you how much they love you, but they never seem able to loan you money. At Minnesota Federal, we love you, too, but we also have money to loan . . . at very competitive rates.
Banker 3: I can't give you anything but love.
(SFX: Music up)
Anncr: VO: Minnesota Federal. Money to loan without the song and dance.

Keep on Knockin'
30 Seconds
(Music intro under)
Anncr: VO: When it comes to
borrowing money, some banks make you
feel a little unwelcome.
**(Music: Little Richard's "Keep a
Knockin'")**
Anncr: VO: Next time, come to
Minnesota Federal. With millions of
dollars to lend, our doors are always open.

Hit the Road Jack
30 Seconds
Anncr: Does it seem like the only time
your bank isn't happy to see you is when
you want to borrow money?
**(Music: "Hit the Road Jack" comes
up and continues)**
Anncr: VO: Next time, come to
Minnesota Federal. With millions of
dollars to lend, we're not about to tell
you to take a walk. Minnesota Federal.

Minnesota
Federal
The Plain Talk Bankers.

Rolling Stone

Founded during the tumultuous 1960s, Rolling Stone magazine was among the first "aboveground" publications to take the visual vocabulary, and at least some of the philosophy, of the counterculture underground press and introduce them to mainstream publishing. As such, it became closely associated with other social phenomena of the era: "flower children," peace marches, rock concerts and campus activism. As the generation of Americans that made up Rolling Stone's primary audience changed, however, its reputation with media buyers and advertisers did not. Despite the fact that Rolling Stone reader surveys revealed that the magazine's primary audience was affluent enough to be buying new cars and other expensive items, advertisers who manufactured these products generally stayed out of the magazine because of lingering perceptions of the Rolling Stone image. It fell to art director Nancy Rice and copywriter William Miller of Fallon McElligott Rice to bring these advertisers and the advertising community as a whole up-to-date. "We wanted to change the perception of the magazine among media decision-makers in order to create a more positive environment for advertising sales," Miller says. "We also wanted to establish a distinctive long-term position for Rolling Stone magazine among the advertising trade."

The resulting campaign is sure to open the eyes of anyone who still thinks of Rolling Stone as a holdout from the '60s. Each of the ads uses a double-page spread format to illustrate Rolling Stone's past, labelled "Perception," and its present, called "Reality." For example, one ad presents under "Perception" a photograph of a long-haired, beaded and bearded "flower child." On the opposite page, under "Reality," is a photo of a clean-cut, neatly-dressed "yuppie." Another ad addresses car advertisers with a psychedelically painted VW van under "Perception," contrasting that with a sleek imported sports car labelled "Reality." The most provocative ad of the campaign, however, is one that features a photo of liberal presidential candidate George McGovern under "Perception," and a picture of Ronald Reagan under "Reality," vividly illustrating how much Rolling Stone's audience has presumably veered to the right.

One might imagine that the campaign, which first appeared in advertising trade magazines in June 1985, would offend some of the magazine's long-time readers—especially if they recall with sympathy some of the icons it mocks. "We haven't heard much in the way of reaction from readers," Miller says, "which is probably due to the fact that it is a trade campaign. Reaction in the trade, however, has been considerable. Rolling Stone has experienced an 18 per cent increase in advertising pages, and a 30 per cent increase in ad sales revenues."

Client: Rolling Stone
Agency: Fallon McElligott Rice, Minneapolis
Art director: Nancy Rice
Copywriter: William Miller
Photography: Mark Hauser (flower child/yuppie), Marvy Photography (cars, shoes), Rolling Stone (Jimi Hendrix), Newsweek (George McGovern), Time-Life (Ronald Reagan)

Perception.

Reality.

If your idea of a Rolling Stone reader looks like a holdout from the 60's, welcome to the 80's. Rolling Stone ranks number one in reaching concentrations of 18-34 readers with household incomes exceeding $25,000. When you buy Rolling Stone, you buy an audience that sets the trends and shapes the buying patterns for the most affluent consumers in America. That's the kind of reality you can take to the bank.

Source: Simmons 1984

Perception.

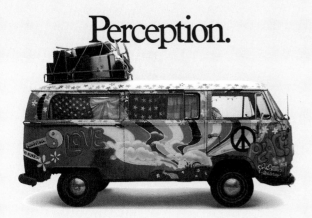

Reality.

If you still think a Rolling Stone reader's idea of standard equipment is flowers on the door panels and incense in the ashtrays, consider this: Rolling Stone households own 5,199,000 automobiles. If you've got cars to sell, welcome to the fast lane. Source: Simmons 1984

Rolling Stone ®

Perception.

George McGovern

Reality.

If you still think Rolling Stone readers are taking left turns when the rest of the world is taking rights, consider who they voted for in the last election. The winner. Source: Audits and Surveys 1984

Rolling Stone ®

Perception.

Reality.

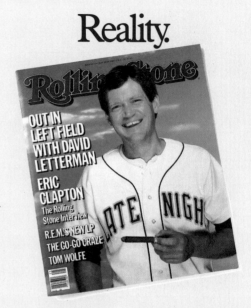

If you think the pages of Rolling Stone are filled with left wing politics and music to make your hair stand on end, call 1-212-758-3800 and we'll send you a copy of America's #1 lifestyle publication for 18-34 year olds, featuring the latest and most respected information about what's happening in music and entertainment today. If you're not on the cover of Rolling Stone, don't worry, there's still room inside. Source: Simmons 1984

Perception.

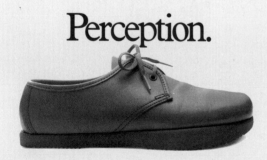

Reality.

If you still think Rolling Stone readers are walking around with their heels on the wrong end of their shoes, consider this: Rolling Stone readers spent over 24 million dollars on athletic footwear last year. Put your best foot forward in Rolling Stone. Source: Simmons 1984

Amtrak

Created from 13 separate railroads by an Act of Congress in 1971, Amtrak struggled for years with antiquated and often under-maintained equipment. As a result, this last vestige of the once proud passenger rail service found itself losing business to the more modern and more comfortable airlines and buses. Beginning in 1977, the railroad underwent a six-year retooling program that was to take six years and resulted in equipment and facilities that rivalled those of its major competitors, the airlines, for comfort and reliability. Market research conducted by Amtrak's agency, Needham Harper Worldwide, revealed that, even by 1983, the travelling public *still* perceived the railroad as having antiquated, uncomfortable equipment, poor on-time performance, and a limited number of destinations. In short, the public was unaware of Amtrak's massive improvement campaign. "Since many of these negative impressions were no longer true," says Needham creative director Michael Robertson, "the advertising became a simple matter of stating the facts and using air travel as the gold standard."

The result of Robertson's approach is an aggressive print campaign that not only addresses the widely held misperceptions of Amtrak, but is also bold enough to compare train travel on Amtrak with air travel. One ad in this campaign features a collection of baggage tags representing major metropolitan airports, and a copy line boasting, "We go to more places than all the airlines combined." The body copy elaborates by pointing out that Amtrak serves 475 cities, some of which may be too small to have an airport, but not too small to have a train station. Another ad features a photograph of one of Amtrak's sleek new locomotives, and touts the comfort of Amtrak's wide seats over the narrower ones used by airlines. It even dares to suggest: "Maybe your

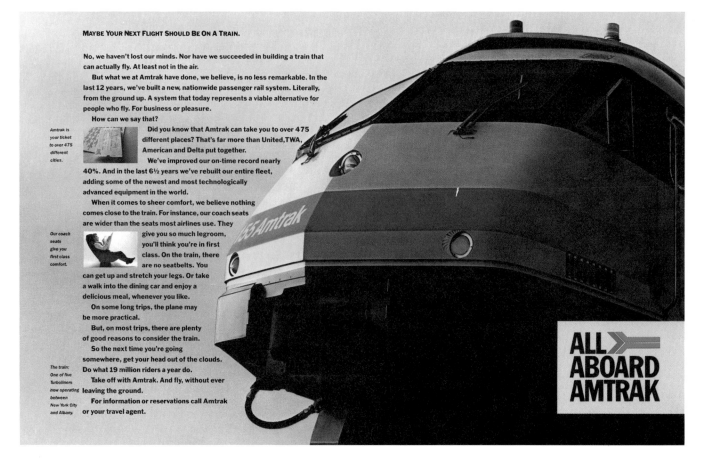

next flight should be on a train." All the ads stress Amtrak's improved on-time performance and amenities—such as rental cars and hotels—available at a traveller's destination.

Robertson says that publicizing Amtrak's improvements without comparisons to air travel was considered, "but the client agreed that doing so would have taken the teeth out of the advertising." Nonetheless, he continues, the campaign "held back" on some issues. "Some of the claims we could have made," he says, "though true, were considered too damaging to air travel to use." Robertson declined to offer any examples, saying, "It was never our intention to make war on the airlines."

One reason for the campaign's relative restraint may have been that Amtrak didn't have the budget to wage "war" with its skyborne rivals. Robertson points out that Amtrak spends only five per cent of what the air travel industry spends on advertising, and only four per cent of what the mass transportation industry overall spends. "Although," he notes, "using as many spreads as we did overcame some of that deficit."

The campaign ran from February of 1983 to February of 1984 in newspapers and in consumer and trade magazines. The ads are credited with producing a 14 per cent increase in "positive perceptions of Amtrak," as well as an eight per cent increase in ridership and a 22 per cent increase in revenue.

Client: National Railroad Passenger Corp. (Amtrak)
Agency: Needham Harper Worldwide, Inc., New York City
Art directors: Bob Cox, Paul Frahm
Copywriter: Michael Robertson
Photography: William Troy (baggage tags), Amtrak stock (train, ticket), stock (swan)

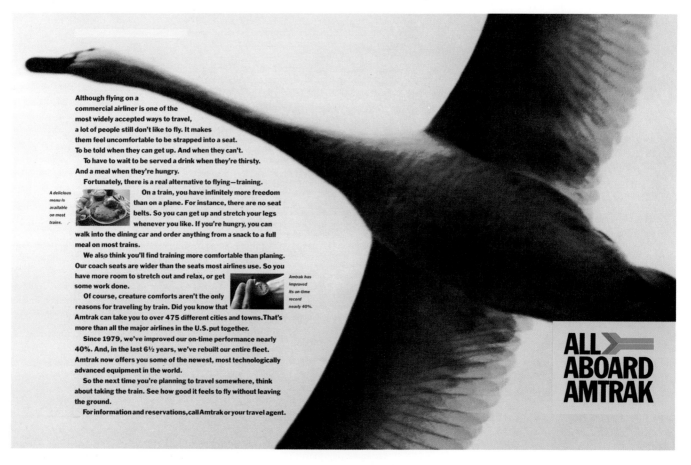

Although flying on a commercial airliner is one of the most widely accepted ways to travel, a lot of people still don't like to fly. It makes them feel uncomfortable to be strapped into a seat. To be told when they can get up. And when they can't.

To have to wait to be served a drink when they're thirsty. And a meal when they're hungry.

Fortunately, there is a real alternative to flying—training.

A delicious menu is available on most trains. On a train, you have infinitely more freedom than on a plane. For instance, there are no seat belts. So you can get up and stretch your legs whenever you like. If you're hungry, you can walk into the dining car and order anything from a snack to a full meal on most trains.

We also think you'll find training more comfortable than planing. Our coach seats are wider than the seats most airlines use. So you have more room to stretch out and relax, or get some work done.

Of course, creature comforts aren't the only reasons for traveling by train. Did you know that *Amtrak has improved its on-time record nearly 40%.* Amtrak can take you to over 475 different cities and towns. That's more than all the major airlines in the U.S. put together.

Since 1979, we've improved our on-time performance nearly 40%. And, in the last 6½ years, we've rebuilt our entire fleet. Amtrak now offers you some of the newest, most technologically advanced equipment in the world.

So the next time you're planning to travel somewhere, think about taking the train. See how good it feels to fly without leaving the ground.

For information and reservations, call Amtrak or your travel agent.

ALL ABOARD AMTRAK

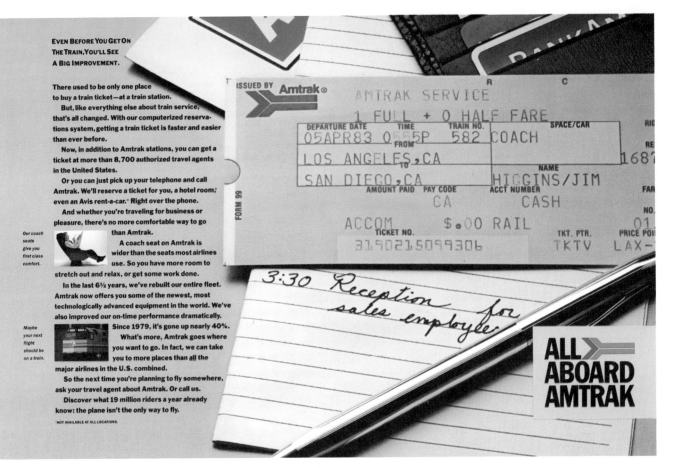

Gotcha Surfwear

The key to Gotcha Sportswear's success among the country's surfing and beach community is "being innovators in the industry and staying ahead of everyone else," says Dwight Smith, designer with Salisbury Communications. "So our advertising for them has to be the same way." Smith says one of the ways his firm "stays ahead" is by "switching techniques": He points out that the hand-painted photography phase of Salisbury's ongoing campaign for Gotcha, presented here, is a combination of techniques from two earlier

phases. "Before we ran this group," he explains, "we used a straight photographic technique. And before that, we used straight illustration."

Smith further notes that the hand-colored photography is an effort to lend an "artsy feel" to Gotcha's products, an approach that has its most literal expression in the ad featuring two of the scene's four models posing as paintings on a wall. Another ad seems to be a visual expression of the client's name "Gotcha," as it depicts three men with thumbs and index fingers poised as mock pistols,

leaning over a woman dramatically draped on a couch in a manner suggesting that she has just been "shot." The third ad in the group represents another approach that is used throughout the campaign: that of using professional surfers, familiar to the ads' target group, as models. This particular example features pro surfer Mark Potter posing in a pair of bright yellow shorts, with his popular nickname, "Potts," written across the background in smeared paint.

This phase of the campaign ran in surfing magazines for five

months, and though Smith says that neither Salisbury Communications nor Gotcha conducts research to determine the campaign's effect on sales, he does note that sales for Gotcha Surfwear "continue to go up."

Client: Gotcha Sportswear
Agency: Mike Salisbury Communications, Inc., Lomita, CA
Art director: Mike Salisbury
Designer: Dwight Smith
Photographer: Michael Russ (Potts), Steve Harvey (Gotcha, paintings)
Hand-coloring: Terry Lamb

This 30-second spot created by BBDO to introduce a new line of Black and Decker consumer power tools, the M47 Series, is a literal execution of a remark made by a member of a focus group conducted by Black & Decker to determine consumer preferences on the new tools. "A professional carpenter told them that when he was really comfortable with a tool, it felt like an 'extension of his own hand,'" explains copywriter Eliot Riskin. "So we came up with the line 'works with your hand as if it were one.'"

Indeed, the commercial shows just that: a man's bare hand working as a power tool, drilling, cutting and sanding. As each function is demonstrated, however, the man's finger is replaced by the appropriate power tool. "We had considered a more introductory approach that would have explained how the tools were developed," Riskin says, "but we wanted an image that would break through viewer resistance and portray the products as state-of-the-art."

Aimed at males aged 24 to 54 years old, the spot began appearing on both broadcast and cable television nationally in May 1985, and on into 1986.

Client: Black & Decker
Agency: BBDO, New York City
Art director: Gunnar Skillins
Copywriter: Eliot Riskin
Agency producers: Jerry Cammisa, Alice Chevalier
Production company: Bean Kahn with Dream Quest, New York City
Director: Jim Spencer

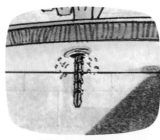

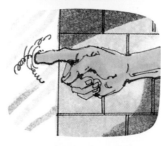

Storyboard and finished commercial.

Hands
30 Seconds
Anncr: VO: Black & Decker introduces a revolution in power tool technology. A line of tools designed specifically to work as one with your hand. The M47 Series. Smaller, more compact, for better control and greater accuracy. And driven by the most powerful motor for its size we've ever built. The M47 Series power tools. They work with your hand as if they were one. From Black & Decker. Ideas at work.

Knox Lumber

"You have a mission to accomplish," says the tense, terse voiceover. On the screen, chrome flashes in the semi-darkness while sparks fly from a butane torch. "You need the right tools," the voiceover continues as the sound of metal against metal rings in the background, "the right materials. You need"—the voiceover pauses dramatically while on the screen a huge door opens and admits a blinding stream of sunlight—"the right stuff." And emerging from the darkness we see, not an astronaut equipped for space flight, but a suburban homeowner burdened with every tool imaginable for routine home maintenance. "Knox," the voiceover concludes. "All the right stuff at all the right prices."

So goes the tongue-in-cheek, 30-second spot for Knox Hardware, a Minnesota-based discount hardware chain. Created by copywriter Jarl Olsen and art director Pat Burnham of Fallon McElligott Rice, the idea was, according to Olsen, "simply to sell Knox as a place that had everything in the way of home supplies and sold them cheaply." "We got the idea from Pat," Olsen explains, "who tries to do menial tasks around his suburban home. He says a handyman needs more heavy metal equipment than an astronaut."

The spot ran throughout Minnesota during all of 1985, and though Olsen says no sales increase has been attributed to it, consumer reaction has been enthusiastic. "People have liked this spot so much that they've written fan letters," he reports.

Client: Knox Lumber
Agency: Fallon McElligott Rice, Minneapolis
Art director: Pat Burnham
Copywriter: Jarl Olsen
Agency producer: Judy Carter
Production company: Wilson Griak, Minneapolis
Director: Eric Young

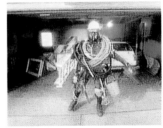

Right Stuff
30 Seconds
(SFX: Snap sounds, like small explosions, electronic hum)
Anncr: VO: You have a mission to accomplish. **(Continue SFX)** You need the right attitude.
(SFX: Chains)
Anncr: VO: The right tools.
(SFX: Torch being lit)
Anncr: VO: The right materials.
(SFX: Skill saw)
Anncr: VO: You need the right stuff.
(SFX: Metal against metal)
Anncr: VO: Where do you get it?
(SFX: Rumble)
Anncr: VO: Knox. All the right stuff at all the right prices.
(SFX: Birds singing, dogs barking)
Woman's voice (off-camera): John, be careful.

Why Vote?

As a part of its public service contribution, Young and Rubicam has a long tradition of creating nonpartisan election-year advertising exhorting eligible citizens to exercise their right to vote in national elections. "Young and Rubicam has striven over the years to publically fight the popular notion that one person's vote doesn't count," explains Jerry Roach, art director with the agency's New York office. "We believe that if enough good men and women stood by and did nothing, our nation would soon succumb to evil forces."

The ad from that series presented here was created for the 1984 national elections and ran in newspapers nationwide on November 5th, the day before the elections were held. Created by Roach and copywriter Joe Lovering, the ad attempts to address head-on what the two men felt was a significant factor in America's 20-year decline in electoral participation. "After wrestling with the issue and discussing it with other people," Roach recalls, "we began to sense that it was more than just a question of lousy odds—'How can my vote make a difference? It's just a drop in the Atlantic Ocean.' It was also a problem born of a deep cynicism regarding politicians and our political system. People not only felt politicians as a lot were ineffective, but that they were harmless as well. We reasoned that if we could graphically demonstrate the truth that politicians had indeed made a difference, for good as well as evil, then at least one barrier between a person and a voting booth might be eliminated."

The creatives found conveying that idea in an ad a daunting task, as "endless" executions were worked up and rejected as not satisfactorily addressing the issue. One of these, a photograph of a World War II troop ship arriving in Europe, with the headline "America is a place where people will cross the ocean to fight for democracry, but not cross the street to vote," nearly became the finished ad, despite the fact that, in Roach's words, "it introduced the side issue of war and did not reflect a contemporary situation." "We liked that idea the best of all the ones we had generated to that point," Roach explains, "although we still had not solved the problem to our own satisfaction. We were asked to take one last look at the problem before giving up completely, so Joe and I sat down, and in a moment of clarity, almost simultaneously blurted out the ad idea."

The phrase that the creative team "blurted out" was "Politicians are all the same," which became the ad's headline. Later, "Why vote?" was added to clarify the thought, and the visual, which had been portraits of strictly American leaders, was changed to include foreign heads-of-state both past and

Vote Tuesday, Nov. 6
YOUNG & RUBICAM

If Your Voice Goes Unheard, Others Will Choose Your Leaders.

Vote Tuesday, November Sixth.

YOUNG & RUBICAM, INC.

present. "We wanted to do a double-page spread that would have included 100 portraits," Roach says. "But the cost would have been prohibitive, to say the least."

The final ad, as it appears here, consists of portraits of 25 heads-of-state ranging from the admired to the abhorred. Also included is a third category of leader, key to the intent of the ad, which Roach characterizes as "people whose impact is still uncertain, either because the jury is still out on them or because they may be unknown to the reader." "We hoped that people's curiosities would be sparked enough for them to do a little research on their own," Roach explains. "The possibility that debate could be inspired over the relative merits of some politicians also intrigued us, but we primarily wanted people to decide for themselves the value of each politician depicted. We wanted to avoid making a political statement of our own, and by mixing it up and adding a few lesser known figures, we hoped to avoid stacking the deck."

No figures are available on the ad's effect on the 1984 voter turnout, but account supervisor Mark Strook says he received hundreds of phone calls from people who had seen the ad. "All of them," he says, "were complimentary." He also says that the agency plans to run the ad again just before the next national election in 1988.

Agency: Young & Rubicam, New York
Art director: Jerry Roach
Copywriter: Joe Lovering
Photography: Various stock houses and New York Public Library art files

Above and opposite page: Comps representing executions of early ideas. Following page: Finished ad.

"Why vote? Politicians are all the same."

It's a weak excuse for not voting.

Though it's far easier to look back at what has been than to chart the course of what will be, history has proven that all politicians are not quite the same.

And the countries they lead are never quite the same again. **YOUNG & RUBICAM INC.**

Vote Tuesday, Nov. 6